CHICKEN RUN

HATCHING THE MOVIE

BY BRIAN SIBLEY

SCREENPLAY BY KAREY KIRKPATRICK
STORY BY PETER LORD AND NICK PARK
DIRECTED BY PETER LORD AND NICK PARK
PRODUCED BY PETER LORD, DAVID SPROXTON,
AND NICK PARK

Foreword by Mel Gibson

HARRY N. ABRAMS, INC., PUBLISHERS

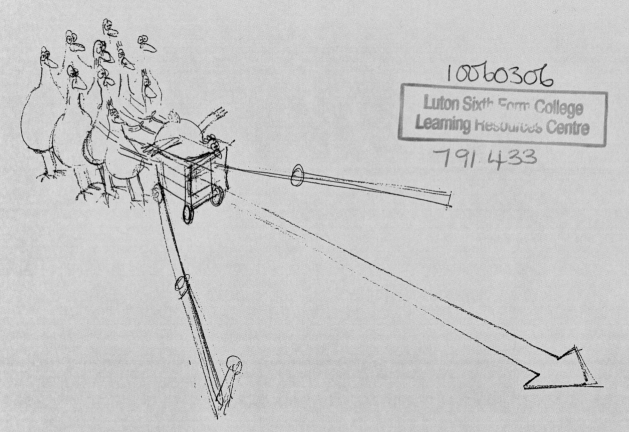

DESIGNER:
Ellen Nygaard Ford, Harry N. Abrams, Inc.

ART DIRECTOR:
Paul Elliott, DreamWorks

Page 1: Sketch of the flying machine by Michael Salter.
Page 2: Animator Jay Grace preps a dog puppet.
This spread: Sketches of chickens by Nick Park.

Library of Congress Cataloging-in-Publication Data
Sibley, Brian.
    Chicken run : hatching the movie / by Brian Sibley ;
foreword by Mel Gibson.
    p.   cm.
    ISBN 0–8109–4124–4
    1. Chicken run (Motion picture). I. Title
PN1997.C464235 S57 2000
791.43'72—dc21   00–27964

Published in 2000 by Harry N. Abrams, Incorporated, New York

Printed and bound in the United States of America

ABRAMS Harry N. Abrams, Inc.
100 Fifth Avenue
New York, N.Y. 10011
www.abramsbooks.com

 Aardman.   PATHÈ!   DreamWorks.

Contents

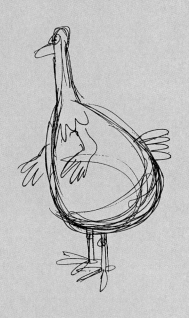

FREEEEEEE

Foreword

By Mel Gibson

In *Chicken Run,* I'm the voice of Rocky. Rocky's body is made of plasticine and silicon and steel. That makes him sound like some kind of high-tech animatronic figure, but that's wrong. The fact is, folks, that Rocky is . . . a puppet. At twelve-inches tall, he's all rooster. The only young rooster in a coop full of pretty sweet chicks, including Ginger, the hen of his dreams. It's a rooster meets hen, rooster falls in love, rooster loses hen kind of story, with a happy ending.

7

In Chicken Run, *Rocky suddenly appears out of the blue. Life on Tweedy's Farm will never be the same again.*

I did the movie because I've always been an admirer of Nick Park and Peter Lord and their studio, Aardman Animations, in Bristol, England. Their gift is to take plasticine and make it come alive, make it walk and talk. I have no idea how they got the idea of making a movie about chickens escaping from a farm that's run like a POW camp. None of the crew is old enough to remember World War II. But then, none of them are chickens, either. Inspiration comes in mysterious ways. I thought the whole concept was pretty funny.

And it was amazing to see how it all came together. The film looks really glossy—the chicken puppets in their super-realistic sets with dramatic lighting are atmospheric and very cool. It's rather like one of those old war movies with soldiers pulling capers in the blue moonlight. This book reveals the years of ingenuity and painstaking artistry that went into achieving these incredible effects.

As for me, I didn't have to work very hard at all. It was a piece of cake. I came through with nothing more serious than a broken arm . . . er, wing.

The opportunity to study this circus poster prop reveals details scarcely glimpsed on screen, such as the times of performances on the "Grand Northern Tour" and the show's name: Col. Daniel Spoon's Travelling Circus— a joke on Western-style circuses and the American folk hero Daniel Boone. The poster was designed by storyboard artist Michael Salter and graphic artist John Davey.

Introduction

It is night in the chicken run. Vicious-looking dogs patrol the perimeter fence. Farmer Tweedy checks the padlock on the gates and sweeps a torch-beam across the rows of huts. All is still and silent. Except for one lone chicken, called Ginger, who slips out of the shadows and begins digging her way under the wire with a kitchen spoon. . . . It is but one of many unsuccessful escape attempts by the chickens of Tweedy's Farm, and it is clear that they will not find it easy to fly the coop. . . .

Thus begins a comedy of crazy escapades, madcap adventures, and daring exploits starring a troupe of—*chickens!* It is August 1999, and I am in Bristol, England, at Aardman Animations, viewing early footage for *Chicken Run,* the studio's first-ever feature film. More than two and a half years of work have already gone into the movie, which uses the studio's painstaking technique of model animation—also called stop-motion animation—featuring puppets made out of plasticine, a compound of clay mixed with oil and wax that has been a popular art material for generations of kids.

With only ten months to go until *Chicken Run* opens as a potential box-office blockbuster, the film's co-directors, Peter Lord and Nick Park, are so busy working to get the film finished on schedule that they scarcely have time to take stock of how much has been achieved since the project began. In the last two years, Aardman Animations has grown from a small company, priding itself on creating animated films with a distinctively "handmade" look, into an organization that currently engages the talents of 150 artists, model makers, animators, and technicians, alongside its regular 80 employees.

The studio where the feature is being made is an anonymous-looking box, situated in a business park a few miles outside the city. Outwardly, the building is as characterless as those occupied by all the other companies on a sprawling site with the exotic title, Aztec West. Inside, however, everything is characteristically Aardmanesque.

There's a corridor-long "rogues' gallery" of wackily posed employee photographs and a more conventional display of glossy pictures of the actors whose voices feature on the film's soundtrack, including one of Mel Gibson confronting his character: Rocky, the Rhode Island Red—or "Rocky Rhodes" for short ("Catchy, ain't it?"). Department doors are eccentrically labeled with multicolored, fridge-magnet-style letters; chicken gags and doodles are pinned up here and there; desks are littered with wind-up toys, fast-food giveaways, and assorted items of merchandise featuring Wallace and Gromit, the "one-man-and-his-dog" stars of the studio's earlier, Academy Award®–winning, short films.

On one wall there's a poster for *Antz* that has been cunningly adapted to feature one of the chickens from Tweedy's Farm; and on another, a framed letter of appreciation from Steven Spielberg, a partner in Hollywood's DreamWorks SKG. The American studio is financing and distributing *Chicken Run* in partnership with French-based Pathè, and has provided welcome creative and logistical support to Aardman over the course of the production.

The staff canteen (or commissary) where I meet Peter and Nick is the emotional core of the building: the place where every day, sooner or later, everyone

(including DreamWorks's cofounder, Jeffrey Katzenberg) stands in line for coffee, breakfast, lunch, or supper. Today's lunch menu, written up on a large chalkboard, ranges from obligatory health-conscious choices to reassuring comfort foods with lots of custard or chocolate sauce. The directors eat, alongside their coworkers, at plain wooden tables, seated on second-hand chapel chairs each of which has a useful rack on the back for hymn books and a place underneath to store a kneeler.

It's all very English, unassuming and understated. Looking down on us from the walls, however, are dynamic one-sheet posters advertising some of the year's top Hollywood movies. Reminders that, one day soon, these are exactly the kind of advertisements that will be pasted up for Aardman's forthcoming film.

"What's fun about this," says Nick, "is being in Britain and yet, at the same time, being in the heart of what *is* Hollywood." It is a thought taken up by Peter: "An English film from Bristol getting the full Hollywood treatment. *That* is exciting."

Aardman may not be as big as some of the animation studios of America, but it has notched up plenty of successes—including hundreds of commercials and dozens of short films that have earned many awards—before launching this latest enterprise. What it hasn't had is any previous experience in making a feature-length, model-animated film. But then nor do most other animation studios: only two such films—Tim Burton's *A Nightmare Before Christmas* (1993) and *James and the Giant Peach* (1996)—have been made in recent years, both of them produced under the aegis of the Disney Company. Before those films, you would

Early days: Nick Park (left), holding a model of Ginger, and Peter Lord, working on a sketch of the chickens' flying machine, in 1997. The wall behind them is covered with reference material on chickens and chicken farming.

14

Peter Lord; right, Nick Park with Richard Priestley, second assistant director.

Everyone gathers for meals in the staff canteen.

have to go back several decades in order to find a handful of such pictures that were made mostly in Europe, none of which could be described as commercial hits.

Peter and Nick both admit that they had no idea what they were taking on: creating characters and devising a story that will hold an audience's attention for more than an hour; raising the finance to pay for a hugely ambitious project; finding premises large enough to accommodate the number and size of the sets required for a feature film; assembling a big enough team of animators, craftsmen, and technicians to *make* the film; and then devising a system that would enable two directors to guide the efforts of more than twenty groups of people, all of whom are simultaneously engaged on different sequences of the film.

And all that doesn't even take into account the daily task of figuring out answers to a hundred unforeseen questions that might range from how chickens dance to the least painful way of constructing several hundred yards of miniature barbed-wire.

As they grapple with the task of completing the film, to budget, on time, they admit that if, when they began, they had

known what they know now, they might never have embarked on it. But they *did*, and with the support, combined energies and devoted efforts of everyone at the studio, they will have made a film that is true to their vision.

"Our pictures," reflects Peter, "are their own thing. They really aren't like other animated films. Why? Because by using models they are, for some reason, more real, more believable than drawn characters."

"We look as though we're a terribly low-tech, handmade, cottage industry," says Nick, "and compared to animators working in cartoons or computer graphics, it might seem as if all we're doing is playing around with plasticine. And yet, that is also the very reason why audiences respond to what we do. Not only can they can see exactly how the animation's done, but because they understand the material we work in—because they've actually handled plasticine, played with it, and know how tactile it is—they say, 'Now, that's *really* clever.'"

What's equally clever are their plots (fast paced and wildly inventive) and their memorable characters. It also doesn't hurt that this film—the story of chickens trying to escape from a farm that is like nothing so much as a prison camp in a POW movie—is really *funny*.

In the darkened screening room, after lunch, the directors run the film for me. It is still very much a work-in-progress: although many sequences are fully animated, others that are still to be filmed are represented on screen by computer visualizations or rough story sketches. However, it is easy to see what they are getting at . . .

The corridor-long "rogues gallery" displays employee photographs.

"Multis" is short for Multiples, the department that makes all the parts of the chickens and assembles them.

One studio tradition is the holding of occasional humorous award ceremonies for staff members. Another is the blackboard showing fun facts about Chicken Run.

An escape movie—with chickens!

Life isn't good for the chickens on Mr. and Mrs. Tweedy's Farm, but Ginger has a vision of what it might be like if she and the others could escape the tyrannical regime under which they live. If they can only get through, under, or over the wire fence, Ginger is sure they will find freedom and a better way of living.

However, every attempt they make goes badly awry. Then, out of the wild blue yonder comes Rocky the Flying Rooster, a smooth-talking American bird on the run from a circus who, in return for a place to hide, agrees to teach the chickens to fly.

Ginger and her companions decide to entrust their fate to Rocky, despite dire warnings from the farm's elderly, resident cockerel, Fowler, who is constantly reminiscing about his days in the Royal Air Force and who has severe reservations about the interloping Yank.

Unable to admit that he cannot actually "fly," Rocky plays for time by organizing intensive training sessions. With the chickens concentrating on other things, egg-production falls and Mrs. Tweedy looks for alternative methods of making money. The arrival of a huge pie-making machine is a sign that—for the chickens— time is running out.

Through a series of desperate exploits, Rocky and Ginger succeed in temporarily disabling the machinery, and the chickens prepare to make their final bid for freedom under Rocky's leadership. It is then that they discover that Rocky is only a Flying Rooster because, in his circus days, he was shot out of a cannon, and that his fortuitous arrival among them was the result of nothing more than a mishap. Incapable of facing failure, Rocky leaves under cover of night.

With the pie machine almost repaired and ready for action, the chickens finally devise a possible means of escape—their own aircraft, scratch built and flown by Fowler, the R.A.F. veteran.

As they prepare to take to the air and the Tweedys attempt to foil their get-away, Rocky returns to play his own heroic part in the daring escape which ensues . . .

19

Inspirational artwork (by Michael Salter and Warwick Cadwell-Johnson) showing some of the film's key frames. These pictures were painted in winter 1998 to provide strong visual indication of the film's story and how it would look in discussions with producers and distributors.

The lights come up in the screening room. As Peter and Nick derive some amusement from pointing out, there is a passing parallel between the experiences of the filmmakers and those of the characters whose destiny is described in *Chicken Run*.

"You see," laughs Nick Park, "we are a bit like those chickens. They know precisely what they *want* to do, they have vision and plenty of enthusiasm but—to start with, at any rate—they really don't have the faintest idea how to actually *do* it." Peter Lord takes up the theme: "And you could go further and say that not only are the chickens a bunch of incompetent birdbrains but it takes an American to come in and sort them all out. *Except* that the smooth-talking American turns out to be a complete fraud." He pauses a moment, then adds, "I mean, *in the film*, of course."

21

It is a notion that sums up these two men: a self-effacing modesty, jostling with a taste for irreverence and flashes of irony. But it is their confidence in what they do and their experience in doing it supremely well that allowed the film company on the west coast of England to forge a strong creative relationship with a film company on the west coast of the United States. That collaborative relationship has resulted in the story and images we have just seen. In the pages that follow we tell how that story was put onto film.

Rocky's American charm makes a strong impression on the inmates of Hut 17 — with the exception of the skeptical Ginger. Featured in this shot are superbly made props (such as an oil lamp, a candle in a jam jar, and a spool of thread) all carefully scaled to a chicken-sized world.

ROCKY: . . . and the pig says to the horse, 'Hey fellah, why the long face!?' AH HA HA HA!!!

PLAN H

B

A

45°

25 yds

Part 1 The Coop

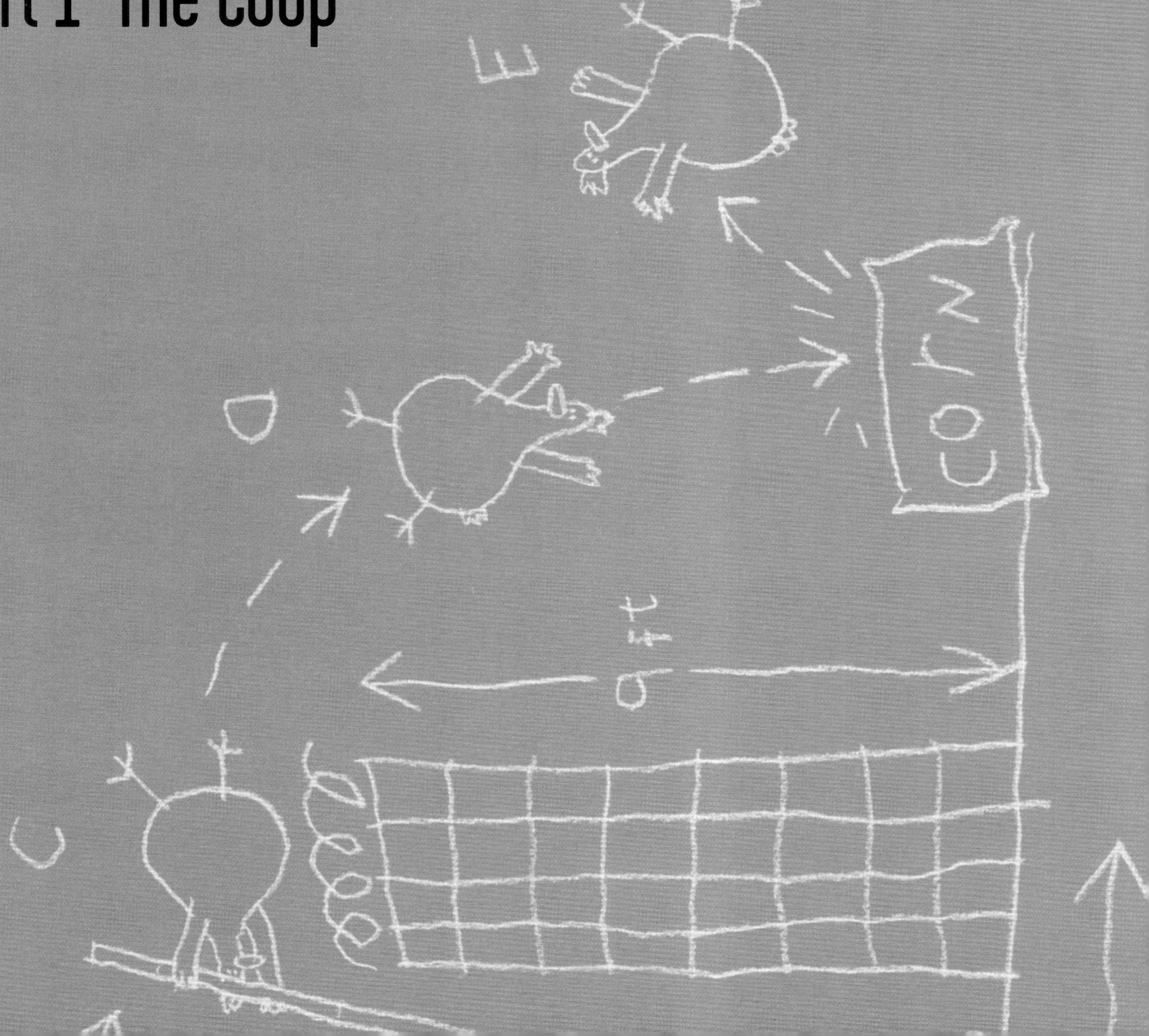

In an animated film, it takes time to make even the simplest joke. For example, Ginger is just out of solitary confinement and is welcomed back by Mac, the bespectacled Scottish chicken, who asks Ginger if she has come up with a new escape plan. The script for *Chicken Run* explains what happens next:

Ginger, keeping a watchful eye trained on Mrs. Tweedy, secretly slips Mac a folded scrap of paper. Mac discreetly unfolds it, lowers her glasses, eyes it. Looks confused.

MAC: I thought we tried going under.

Ginger quickly reaches over, flips the drawing upside down.

MAC: Ah! Over! Right!

It is a small, passing, moment in the film, but one which amusingly reinforces not only Ginger's resourcefulness but also her problems in communicating with some of her feathered comrades. Fleeting though the scene is, it involved many days work for one of the film's animators. But the Aardman philosophy is quite simple: if a scene needs to be in the film—in order to help us understand the plot or a character's motivation, or just to make us laugh—then it will be in the film, regardless of what problems have to be overcome in creating that scene in animation.

"We don't make 'animated films,'" says Peter Lord emphatically. "We make FILMS—and, by the way, they happen to be animated."

"Ladies, please. Let's not lose our heads." **GINGER**

Since they *are* animated, it follows that nothing we see in the film truly takes place: Ginger never uses a garden gnome to fend off a snarling dog; Rocky never lounges in a chicken-made Jacuzzi sipping a "cocktail"; and Babs never knits beak warmers, tea cozies, or flying goggles. It's true that all these moments exist as a series of still photographs, but they never really move.

What we see when we watch *Chicken Run* is nothing more than "a trick of the eye." It is all an optical illusion known as "persistence of vision," which occurs because the human eye retains an image for a fraction of a second after seeing it. And if—in that moment—one image can be switched for another that is slightly different, then the eye is cheated into thinking that it has seen the first image move.

This is what is happening whenever we sit in a cinema, regardless of whether we are watching an animated film or one made in live action. What we see on the screen are not, in fact, moving pictures at all, but simply a long strip of still pictures whizzing past our eyes so fast—twenty-four of them every second—that we are fooled into believing that those pictures are actually moving.

However, what is significantly different about making animated films is that while the live-action movie camera captures real movements in real time—"freezing" them into separate still

pictures, which can then be projected onto a screen—the animator has to create all those movements: whether something as seemingly elementary as a row of chickens shuffling into line for the daily roll call at Tweedy's Farm or an elaborate sequence like the one in which Ginger and Rocky escape from the pie machine.

In short, everything we see in every single frame of an animated film—characters and settings—have to be designed and built from scratch. And, unlike a live-action film where nothing is hidden between one frame of film and the next, an animated film is made up of what we see on screen and a huge amount of unseen work that has gone on in the spaces between the frames where the illusion of movement is created.

Peter Lord explains: "When you start to make a puppet move in model animation, you know where the move starts from but you don't know where it is going to finish, because you haven't got there yet—like real life, come to think of it. So every single stage of the movement is an experiment, or even an adventure—because you have this idea of where you're heading, but no certainty of getting there."

Like a lot of experiments, animating is a slow, painstaking process. It requires not only skill in molding and shaping the models but also intuition, imagination, and inventiveness so that those models

 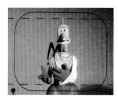   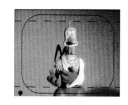 

appear to live and breathe. When done well, an animated performance holds our attention as strongly as that of any actor and—as *Chicken Run* shows—can make us laugh or even move us to tears.

In fact, being an animator is not unlike being an actor. "That is exactly what you are!" agrees supervising animator Loyd Price. "You are making a lump of plasticine act! And people are watching it, reacting to it. The beauty of animation is that you're bringing to life something that is completely inanimate. The whole of filmmaking is the art of illusion, but animation is the ultimate illusion because if you turn the camera off, what you are left with is just a lump of plasticine!"

It is an illusion that has fascinated filmmakers now for over a hundred years and people have been manipulating plasticine (and before that clay) since the earliest days of cinema. In fact one of the first animated film series ever made was entitled *Miracles in Mud.*

The present popularity of the medium, however, owes a lot to the work of Aardman Animations' founders, Peter Lord and David Sproxton, which began to be seen on British television screens in the 1970s.

As schoolboys and then as university students, Peter and David began contributing short animated films to a BBC television program for deaf children called *Vision On.* And it was a character

created for this series—not in plasticine but in drawn animation—who in 1972 gave his name to the fledgling company which might otherwise have been called Sproxton & Lord (or even Lord Sproxton).

Called "Aardman," he was dressed in the standard superhero gear (cape, boots, and underpants worn over tights), although his exploits were decidedly inept and accident prone. Although now long forgotten, "Aardman" lives on, not just in the company name but also in the studio's repeated creation of well-intentioned, but slightly incompetent, characters: Wallace, the would-be inventor of the films *A Grand Day Out, The Wrong Trousers,* and *A Close Shave,* and the tirelessly inventive but invariably misguided escapees in *Chicken Run.*

Peter Lord and David Sproxton's youthful ambitions to animate were fired by the work of established animators such as fantasy filmmaker Ray Harryhausen, who had worked with Willis O'Brien, the genius behind *King Kong* (1933), and whose own pictures combined live-action actors with fabulous animated creatures such as the terrifying army of skeletal warriors in his remarkable film *Jason and the Argonauts* (1963).

Another formative influence was the surreal animation contributed by Terry Gilliam to the ground-breaking television comedy series, *Monty Python's Flying Circus* (1969–74).

Each second of film requires twenty-four frames. The twelve frames below show how movement—in this case, an early test of Rocky turning his head—is broken down over the course of half a second. Incidentally, Rocky's wattle, seen here, was eliminated in the final version of the character.

Morph had a knack of "morphing" into (and out of) different shapes—a dog, a chair, a chest-of-drawers—as well as being able to pass through objects and, at will, revert to being nothing more than a lump of the raw material from which he was made.

Although Gilliam's animation appeared in a sophisticated adult program and Harryhausen's films were popular with all ages of cinema goers, the prevailing attitude at the time was that the primary audience for animation was children. However, the phenomenal popularity with audiences of all ages of Serge Danot's French puppet series, *The Magic Roundabout* (1965), encouraged Peter and David in their belief that animation was

many advertising agencies that began commissioning animated commercials from the fledgling company.

The character, created in 1980, who paved the way to even greater success was Morph, a small, terra-cotta colored plasticine man who interacted with Tony Hart, the presenter of a popular children's television show featuring arts and crafts.

28

not to be dismissed as being simply "kids' stuff." *Chicken Run,* like so much of their work, is proof that they were right. Their partnership went from strength to strength. Peter concentrated on the animation while David took responsibility for the technical side of the filmmaking. After experimenting with various media, they almost exclusively concentrated on working with plasticine. As a medium, plasticine promised more sophistication and flexibility than other forms of puppet animation. Furthermore, since plasticine-model animation was being used by few other studios, Aardman's work seemed refreshingly different to television executives as well as to the

Morph was soon starring in his own television series (1981) featuring an extended family of charmingly zany characters. His simple shape, friendly features, and warm color earned Morph great popularity with the British public and, at the same time, secured the reputation of Aardman Animations.

Particularly imaginative was Morph's use of borrowed household objects—such as match boxes and spools of thread—to furnish and equip his miniature world. The same invention is seen at work in *Chicken Run,* where an old pipe is used as a gavel to call the escape committee to order; where the opportunistic rats, Nick

FETCHER: How 'bout this quality hand-crafted tea set.

NICK: Or this beaut'ful little number, all the rage in the fashionable chicken coops of Paris. Simply pop it on like so and as the French hens say—Voila!

and Fetcher, will try and sell a badminton birdie as a hat; and where Ginger uses a roller skate to move along the escape tunnels and an eggbeater to tunnel under the stockade fence.

Aardman Animations work took a new direction in *Conversation Pieces* (1982) and *Lip Synch* (1989), film series featuring a diversity of situations presented in the style of "fly-on-the-wall" documentaries.

Although to begin with these films recreated fairly faithfully the situations suggested by the dialogue, they began increasingly to use the soundtrack as merely a starting point for something less literal and more imaginative, such as the studio's first Academy Award—winning film, *Creature Comforts* (1989–90), which showed animated zoo

animals speaking the thoughts of real people living in retirement homes and student hostels.

Creature Comforts was created and animated by Nick Park, who had been inspired in his desire to animate by the Morph films of Peter Lord and David Sproxton and who joined the studio in 1985 to complete *A Grand Day Out* (1989), a film project he had begun as a student at the National Film and Television School.

The ingenious chickens put everyday household objects to good use in their desperate quest for freedom: pulled along on a roller skate and equipped with a kitchen spoon, Ginger (above) prepares to dig her way out of Tweedy's farm. For Nick and Fetcher, opposite, a badminton birdie substitutes for more glamorous merchandise. The storyboard frames are by Michael Salter.

A bird from the Aardman aviary: Feathers McGraw, a penguin desperado (who sometimes disguises himself as a chicken), tampers with the Techno-Trousers in the 1993 Academy Award–winning film The Wrong Trousers, a picture that hints at the dangers of allowing machines to fall into the wrong hands—or wings. By the way, in his chicken disguise, Feathers looks not unlike . . . Rocky.

The Academy Award–nominated *A Grand Day Out* featured the exploits of Wallace, an eccentric would-be inventor with a passion for cheese, and Gromit, his long-suffering canine companion, who builds a rocket and sets off on a lunar expedition in search of moon-cheese. It was one of an increasing number of films in which the studio demonstrated that it was capable of creating original stories sustaining its storytelling powers for longer than just a few minutes.

Nick Park's two films and Peter Lord's *Adam* (1991)—which was also nominated for an Academy Award—showed a growing sophistication in ability to convey a complex range of human emotions, a talent which is fully realized in *Chicken Run*, where the characters run the gamut of responses from anger, anxiety, sadness, and despair to confidence, compassion, joy, and expectation. The miracle of Aardman's acting skills can be seen particularly in the animation of characters' eyes which—whilst being nothing more than beads set in a lump of plasticine—appear to widen with fear, narrow in anger, or fill with tears of sorrow.

A Grand Day Out generated two highly successful, Academy Award–winning, sequels—*The Wrong Trousers* (1993) and, two years later, *A Close Shave*. Both films, running for a little less than half an hour, displayed the now-familiar hallmarks of a Nick Park picture: unlikely characters and zany situations, presented in a super-realistic style that believably locates their otherwise bizarre scenarios in the world of our own experience.

Aardman's films established a successful narrative formula: strong story lines with sustained emotional development punctuated by elaborately executed animation set-pieces. *The Wrong Trousers,* for example, contains the pathetic scene in which the rejected Gromit (with his worldly belongings wrapped in a spotted handkerchief) leaves home and kennel in a thunderstorm, as well as the thrill-packed sequence in which Wallace, trapped in a pair of fully automated (ex-NASA) Techno-Trousers, is the unwitting stooge in an elaborate diamond heist.

Other popular Aardman ingredients finding their way into the feature film

include themes, jokes, and ideas first explored in the earlier Wallace and Gromit films, such as Babs's obsessive passion for knitting, which reprises a knitting motif established in *A Close Shave* with Wendolene's wool shop. It can hardly be a coincidence that Feathers McGraw, the penguin villain of *The Wrong Trousers,* puts a red rubber glove on his head in order to disguise himself as . . . a chicken. And it is small wonder that the ultimate threat facing the chickens in *Chicken Run* should be represented by the pie machine with which Mrs. Tweedy plans to take the failing farm "out of the middle ages and into full-scale automated production," since machines featured prominently in all three Wallace and Gromit films.

A prime influence on the *Chicken Run* directors was the comic inventions created by the British cartoonist and illustrator, William Heath Robinson, whose career spanned the early years of the twentieth century and whose name—like that of his American counterpart, Rube Goldberg—has passed into the language as a way of describing any complicated machine.

Robinson's whimsical drawings reflect a decidedly English idiom, as does the work of artist and inventor Rowland Emett, who specialized in bizarrely-constructed vehicles and who dreamt up the eccentric gadgetry for Caractacus Potts, Dick Van Dyke's madcap character in the film *Chitty Chitty Bang Bang* (1968). Both artists created machines that had all the appearance of having been put together by a resourceful amateur whose construction methods included liberal use of tape and bits of badly knotted string.

There is also a strongly defined American tradition of nonsensical mechanical devices, represented not only by Goldberg but also by early Hollywood cartoons. In *Plane Crazy,* one of the very first Mickey Mouse films made in 1928, Walt Disney's inventive hero enthralls his barnyard friends by constructing and flying an airplane built out of old crates and planks and powered by a "spring" made from a tightly wound dachshund.

The attraction felt by Nick Park and Peter Lord to this magical vision of technology is understandable, particularly since both directors began their filmmaking in spectacularly unsophisticated ways: cameras lashed to kitchen tables, garden sheds serving as primitive studios. And, as Nick recalls, rather like the gadgetry imagined by Heath Robinson, Emett, and Disney, just about all you needed could be stored in a cardboard box.

"When I was a kid," he reflects, "I used to have what I called 'My Box of Useful Things' which

Gromit (below) was seen to be an enthusiastic knitter in the films The Wrong Trousers *and* A Close Shave, *a passion he shares with Babs in* Chicken Run *(below left). Gromit's co-star, Wallace (above), enjoys a nice slice of toast thickly covered in jam and prepared by his own wacky labor-saving device, the Auto-Jam Ballister.*

31

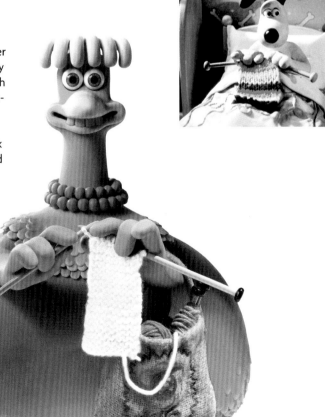

"We were about thirteen or fourteen and we thought his pictures were fantastic," says Peter Lord of William Heath Robinson. "They were drawn so cleverly that you thought, 'Yes! I get it! They would really work!' Even though common sense told you they wouldn't!"

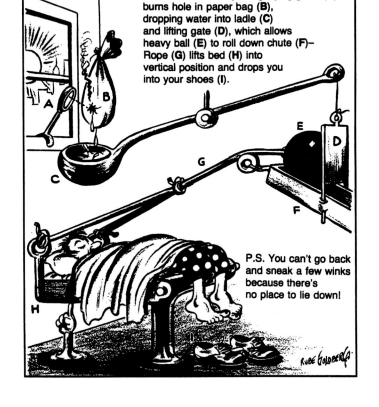

When sun comes up, magnifying glass (**A**) burns hole in paper bag (**B**), dropping water into ladle (**C**) and lifting gate (**D**), which allows heavy ball (**E**) to roll down chute (**F**)— Rope (**G**) lifts bed (**H**) into vertical position and drops you into your shoes (**I**).

P.S. You can't go back and sneak a few winks because there's no place to lie down!

Artistic inspiration for Peter Lord and Nick Park's recurring obsession with way-out machines: left, "The Professor's invention for peeling potatoes," an illustration by the British humorist, William Heath Robinson, for one of Norman Hunter's stories about Professor Branestawm; right, "No More Oversleeping," a mechanical means of getting out of bed devised by the American cartoonist Rube Goldberg.

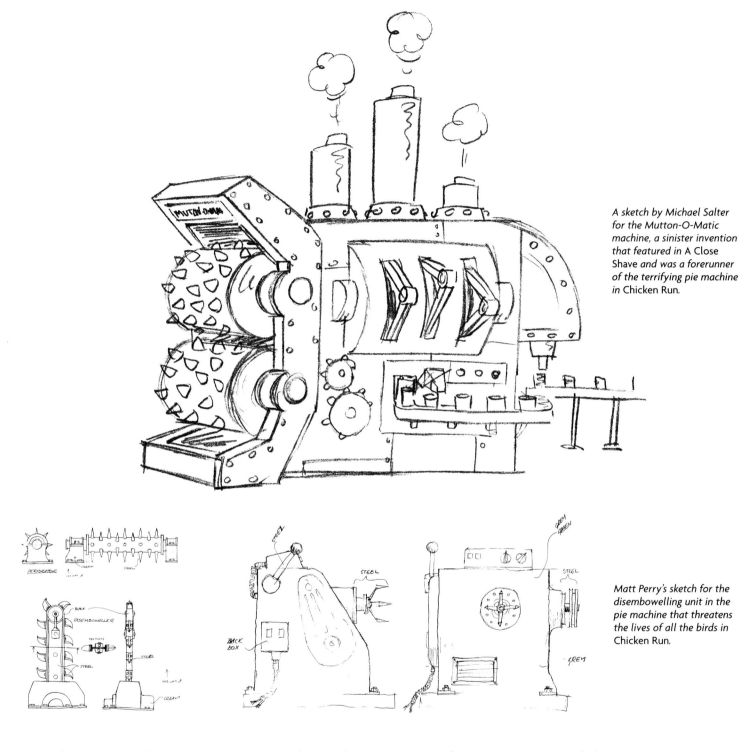

A sketch by Michael Salter for the Mutton-O-Matic machine, a sinister invention that featured in A Close Shave *and was a forerunner of the terrifying pie machine in* Chicken Run.

Matt Perry's sketch for the disembowelling unit in the pie machine that threatens the lives of all the birds in Chicken Run.

Aardman's love-hate relationship with machinery springs from a comic sensibility that has its roots in early live-action comedies as well as graphic and animated cartoons. The machines on this page may be used to create comic scenarios, but they are also dangerously menacing.

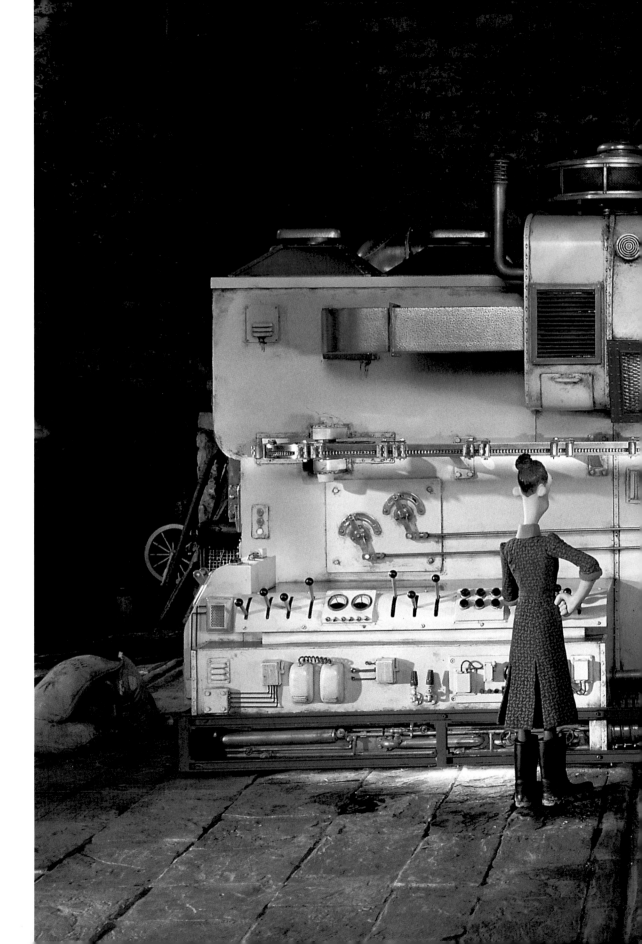

The pie machine in Chicken Run *recalls the immediate postwar years when the aim of contemporary design was to represent progress as the benign servant—rather than the controlling master—of humanity. In reality (or the animated approximation of it) these sleek, shiny surfaces which Nick describes as being "halfway between cartoon and reality" only serve to conceal ruthless dehumanizing—or, in this case, dechickenizing—forces.*

34

I stored under my bed. Bits of old broken toys and motors and clockwork things went into it. And I used to watch films based on the books of H. G. Wells and think, 'One day, I'm going to build myself a time machine or something like that.' And that is the magic of our kind of animation: it's physical. The wonder of it is that it can build anything you can think of and you can actually make it work! You can create a machine where things go in at one end and come out at the other end as something different. You don't have to worry about how the machine does it inside, it's enough that you can see it happen before your eyes!"

A darker strain of skepticism about technology in the work of Park and Lord also has a pedigree. There is a body of work by humorists on both sides of the Atlantic that portrays mechanization as being a threat to man and society. Less than a decade after Mickey had demonstrated his supremely confident—if foolhardy—mastery of his mouse-made aircraft, his cartoon compatriot Donald Duck was seen being overpowered by thirties technology in *Modern Inventions* (1937), a film that itself parodied themes in Charlie Chaplin's *Modern Times* (1936), in which the little tramp grappled with a gargantuan and malevolent machine.

The fear of machines—and particularly those associated with conflict—persisted through the years of the Second World War and into the 1950s. In America, Warner Brother's eternally optimistic Wile E. Coyote was ceaselessly purchasing new contraptions from the celebrated Acme Company to aid him in his tireless pursuit of the elusive Roadrunner, while the French comic filmmaker Jaques Tati became yet another everyman helplessly confronting the machinery of modernity.

Nick Park readily admits to being a part of this long tradition: "Things mechanical have a kind of archaic quality that lends itself to animation. And there is certainly, in our films, a skepticism about technology. If you think in terms of lifestyle and look at all the ridiculous things we invent today, supposedly to make life easier, then *The Wrong Trousers,* for example, seems to be a parable about investing too heavily in a technology that can then take you over."

This ambivalence toward mechanization is evidenced by the fact that *Chicken Run* features two very different mechanical contraptions: the ad-hoc, thrown-together flying machine that—crude though it is—represents freedom; and the automated sleekness of the pie machine symbolizing entrapment and, ultimately, death.

Curious then that, in telling this story—with its implied warning against the soulless march of progress—the studio itself should be making increasing use of the most sophisticated digital technology. There is a strange irony in the fact that the animators are using computers to help them visualize and plan a sequence in which a couple of chickens are trapped inside the diabolical pie machine. But, of course, when it comes to giving movement to those chickens, that calls for good, old-fashioned modeling—the kind of thing small children have done for centuries, going back long before the first machine was ever invented.

With the evil Cyberdog, Preston, at the controls of the Knit-O-Matic machine in A Close Shave *(above), the hapless Wallace and Wendolene (together with a flock of sheep) are plunged into the suds of the washing vat—prior to being dispatched for "shaving." Similar perils face the birds in* Chicken Run *when Mr. Tweedy gets his hands on the controls of the pie machine, opposite.*

37

"When we first discussed the idea for *Chicken Run*," recalls Nick Park, "Pete's reaction was pure *horror*. The idea of a load of characters with spindly legs and fat round bodies that were covered in feathers. I mean it's the opposite of what you would ever want to do in animation."

"Especially," adds Peter Lord, "in *plasticine*. It was an appalling idea. In plasticine, you can't do feathers, you can't do thin legs, and the bodies are going to weigh a ton."

"It's true," admits Nick, "we had chosen the worst possible thing. It was going to be a *complete nightmare.*"

And yet, remarkably, at the point when they are recounting these memories, the nightmare is turning into a dream come true.

The notion that Aardman Animations would, one day, make a feature-length film was practically a foregone conclusion. "The idea," says Peter Lord, "has, in a sense, been around for *ever.*" The only question was: *when*?

Trying to pin down the point at which that idea became a feasible possibility is less easy, since corporate memories are now rather vague on the matter.

Some people remember it being talked about as early as 1990, following the winning of the Academy Award for *Creature Comforts*. Others recall the first serious consideration of such a project starting in 1994, after their second Academy Award, for *The Wrong Trousers*. Certainly the success of that film—which was longer than anything they had yet produced—encouraged the studio to think that since it had been able to sustain story-

"We haven't tried not trying to escape." BUNTY

Lord of the chickens: Peter Lord
in a chicken suit (previous page
and above) and holding a
chicken (below).

telling techniques for a period of almost half an hour, a feature film might now be within their capabilities.

There was talk about making *A Close Shave*, the third film featuring Wallace and Gromit, as a feature. Indeed, if there had been the time and the money to take the finished picture to the full length suggested by the original script and storyboard, it would have had a running time of at least fifty minutes.

Whilst various restraints dictated that *A Close Shave* finally ran at a similar length to *The Wrong Trousers*, it was clear that Aardman's next project would be a feature. The pressing questions now were "what will the film be about?" and, equally important, "where is the money going to come from to make it?"

There was never any doubt that American money was going to be a necessary part of the equation, if only because the studio wanted access to Hollywood distribution and marketing. *A Close Shave* had cost $2.1 million, but a feature would require considerably more than that. "The difference in scale between making a half-hour television film and a full-length theatrical feature," says Peter Lord, "is rather like the difference between building a go-cart and an Aston Martin."

"It was around Academy Awards time in 1994," recalls David Sproxton, "that Hollywood opened its doors." The difficulty was in knowing which doors to enter and what to say and do once inside.

Aardman needed someone to act as a broker between themselves and the

studios of Los Angeles. That person was Canadian producer Jake Eberts, whose Allied Films, an affiliate of the European entertainment company Pathé, had been associated with such Academy Award–winning movies as *Driving Miss Daisy* and *Dances With Wolves*. The former founder and chief executive of Goldcrest Films (responsible for, among many other films, *Chariots of Fire*, *Gandhi* and *The Killing Fields*) had a particular interest in animation, having begun his film career by arranging development financing for the 1974 animated film of *Watership Down*. Eberts's children had introduced him to the films of Wallace and Gromit, and he offered to assist Aardman in its quest for a Hollywood film partner and finance the development of a feature-film idea.

A simple "napkin deal" with Jake Eberts gave Aardman, as executive producer Michael Rose describes it, "the culture in which we could relax and think about ideas." All the major Hollywood studios were interested in working with the three-time Academy Award winners from Bristol and any number of animated projects were proposed and (not too seriously) considered, including proposals for making film versions of various comic-book characters, including Tank Girl.

Whilst literally dozens of legends, fairy-tales, and popular classics were suggested as being ideally suited to receive the Aardman treatment, the studio found it difficult to work up the necessary enthusiasm, mainly because Peter and Nick had, as they put it, a "blind spot" about adapting established stories for the screen.

The answer was—chickens! And why chickens? Well, why not? "They're stupid and ridiculous," says Peter Lord. "I've always liked birds," adds Nick Park, "I like the way they behave and I've always found chickens funny."

A variety of feathered oddballs have appeared in Aardman films, including a group of strange spotted birds from the Academy Award–winning Creature Comforts and a pair of talking penguins who featured in one of the studio's commercials for British electrical appliances.

Nick Park's fascination with chickens dates back to his childhood, growing up in Preston in Lancashire, where he and his sister kept pet chickens. "My sister and I made up stories," recalls Nick, "and we were always coming up with chicken puns such as 'The Lone Free Ranger,' a joke which eventually found its way into the script as a gag for Rocky."

"The trouble was," David Sproxton recalls, "most of the suggestions were simply not us at all. The best stories for us are those which come out of ourselves."

There was, of course, the question of whether such a story might feature the studio's already established characters of Wallace and Gromit. In Britain, the comic duo had achieved the popular status of a national institution, but for a variety of reasons the feeling at the studio was that its first feature should introduce new characters.

So, the question remained: supposing the right Hollywood partner were found, what would Aardman make a feature film about?

At first it wasn't much more than a few doodles of birds in one of Nick's notebooks, where he habitually scribbles down possible visual gags without always knowing how they might eventually be

used. Among the sketches that were now finding their way into its pages was a picture of a chicken trying to dig its way under a fence. "And *there*," says Nick, was the germ of an idea . . . why not make an *escape movie*—with chickens?"

To begin with, Nick had thought of his chicken idea as probably nothing more than a subject for a short film, but as the studio repeatedly found itself rejecting other people's feature proposals it became increasingly apparent that they already had a good one of their own. Various ideas were "in the hat," but the one that made everyone smile the moment they heard it was the one with the chickens.

Peter Lord's first response to the suggestion was somewhat mixed. Obviously it was funny, in the same quirky way as a penguin (disguised as a chicken) planning to steal a priceless diamond is funny. But the prospect of having to animate the birds was terrifying. In the end, however, the sheer wackiness proved totally irresistible and he and Nick were soon coming up with new twists and turns on the idea. "Eventually," says David Sproxton, "we said, 'Hey, let's do this chicken escaping idea!' "

That idea was pitched by Nick, Peter, and Michael to Jake Eberts in January 1996

at the Sundance Film Festival. After the four flew to Los Angeles aboard the DreamWorks jet, they pitched it again over dinner to Steven Spielberg and Jeffrey Katzenberg, who—with David Geffen—had just founded their new studio. Katzenberg had recently left Disney, where he had been responsible for a number of successful films, including the animated feature *The Lion King*.

"It was surreal," recalls Nick, "there really wasn't much to it—all we had was this one joke, 'An escape movie with chickens,' and there I was selling it to Steven Spielberg and Jeffrey Katzenberg. Bizarre!"

The response from the two film moguls was unhesitating. "What a great idea!" said Katzenberg. Spielberg—recognizing, perhaps, that this simplest of story ideas embodied something of his established screen philosophy—was equally encouraging, observing, "I love these chickens so much, I'll never eat another chicken giblet."

Since Jake Eberts was already committed to financing the development of the film via Pathé and no studio money was needed at this point, Katzenberg offered to give his support and advice—with no strings attached. As the principals of Aardman and DreamWorks became comfortable with one another, a

"For two summers, when I was a student," says Nick, "I worked in a chicken-packing factory for about six weeks, in order to earn enough money to buy my first cine camera. One day, I was sent away to work at the slaughterhouse. I drew on those memories for some of the details of the Tweedy's pie machine, such as the way in which the chicken are hung upside down by their legs."

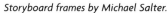

Storyboard frames by Michael Salter.

relationship developed, resulting in an agreement between the two studios and Pathé to co-finance and distribute *Chicken Run,* which was announced in December 1997.

Meanwhile, back in Britain after that first meeting, Nick and Peter locked themselves away for six months devising a rough story line and creating the key characters—including Ginger, Rocky, and Fowler—as well as looking at possible sources of filmic inspiration, of which there were plenty of obvious contenders from both sides of the Atlantic, since the years following the Second World War had seen a proliferation of POW films.

In a view from above, Ginger is seen hanging upside down, her ankles clamped to a conveyor belt that is carrying her toward a chute, where she will be released to fall into the maw of the pie machine.

The chickens assembling for roll call make a poignant scene in a setting that would be evocative to viewers who remember the spate of POW films that were released after the Second World War. In England, for example, Ealing Studio's director, Basil Dearden, made The Captive Heart (1946) a thoroughly British story with a cast headed by Michael Redgrave and Jack Warner. Other POW films, featuring similarly stiff-upper-lip Brits, included The Wooden Horse (1950) with Leo Genn and David Tomlinson and The Colditz Story (1955) starring John Mills. At the same time, in America, Ronald Reagan was making Prisoner of War (1954) and William Holden was starring in Stalag 17 (1953), a film scripted by Billy Wilder and honored in Chicken Run by the fact that Hut 17 on Tweedy's Farm is where the escape committee holds its clandestine meetings. But perhaps the most popularly enduring POW movie was The Great Escape (1963), directed by John Sturges, and featuring a cast of American and British stars headed by Steve McQueen, James Garner, Richard Attenborough, James Donald, Charles Bronson, and Donald Pleasance.

The ceiling of the studio is visible in this photograph of the set, as are some of the lights needed for filming. The optimum size for all of the puppets is between nine and twelve inches high—this is called "A" scale. In scenes such as this one, however, where the chickens interact with human characters, and in wide shots where many chickens appear on a large set, "B" scale chickens are used. These puppets are three to four inches high.

45

   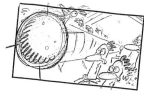 

MAC: Right. We've tried going UNDER the wire and that didnae work. So, the plan is—we go OVER it. This is us, right? We get in like this— wind 'er up—and let 'er go!

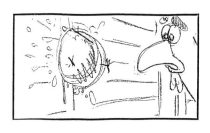

FOWLER: Good grief—the turnip's bought it!

As the story ideas developed it quickly became clear that the film needed to be something more than just a parody of a popular film genre. However amusing audiences might find the initial premise, they would expect a full-length film to deliver something more than mere pastiche. As producer Michael Rose explains, "We needed greater depth and that came from the introduction of thoughts about hope and freedom and what it means to express yourself."

One source of inspiration was *The Song of the Bird*, a book that Nick was reading at the time. A collection of stories, retold by Anthony de Mello from various traditions around the world, it contained a fable entitled "The Golden Eagle."

In this short story—no more than six paragraphs long—a man finds an eagle's egg and places it in a chicken's nest. The egg hatches and the eagle grows up amongst the chickens, assuming that he is also a chicken. He one day sees a great golden eagle soaring through the sky above the yard where he lives, but never flies himself because he believes that he is a chicken—and chickens cannot fly. Eventually he dies, as he has lived, unaware of his true identity.

Even though the fable never did become part of the finished film, *Chicken Run* still contains the theme of a yearning ambition to rise above the limitations imposed by the expectations of others, so that—given the spirit of an eagle— even a chicken might one day fly.

In early versions of the story, as seen in this drawing by Michael Salter, the chickens discover that they can fly if they believe in themselves. Eventually, this idea was dropped.

Opposite, an ingenious scheme is about to be disproved: Ginger watches uncertainly as Mac demonstrates the workings of a possible chicken catapult, wisely using a turnip stand-in. The storyboard frames that show what happens next, seen above, were drawn by Peter Lord.

48

The walls of Hut 17 are covered with diagrams of birdbrained escape plans (drawn by Michael Salter) that are doomed to failure. Plan B, right, calls for the chickens to escape under cover of a feeder and a trough. As executed (above and opposite), the plan flops: Ginger, leading the way in the feeder, scoots through the open gate of the coop only to be pounced upon by Tweedy's dogs; the trough hits the gate sideways and tips over, exposing the chickens.

"The key to writing an animated movie," says *Chicken Run's* screenwriter, Karey Kirkpatrick, "is just to embrace the process and take it one stage at a time. But you really have to pace yourself, because it's a marathon not a sprint!"

It was a lesson that Peter Lord and Nick Park had still to learn when they started developing a script from those first sketchy ideas about a bunch of escaping chickens.

In their early filmmaking days, both men had been responsible for scripting and creating the visual look of their films. Then, when *The Wrong Trousers* was in the planning stage, they decided that they needed the help of a writer. The author of this book worked with Nick in the early development stages of the idea before the film progressed to a script written by Nick in collaboration with Bob Baker, who went on to co-write *A Close Shave*.

Just as *The Wrong Trousers* had represented a quantum leap from the short films that the studio had been making, so *Chicken Run* was going to require the mastering of a whole new set of skills, including the structuring and writing of a feature-length film script.

Much needed to be reconciled, simplified, and developed from the mass of ideas that were already in existence. "We thought about it so much," Peter Lord recalls, "we agonized over the question of whether chickens actually perceived they were in prison or not? After all in a POW movie, you have all these fundamentally honest and heroic people who end up in a prison situation where—not being criminals—they really don't belong. But was it possible to apply this to chickens?"

"Oooh, me life flashed before me eyes. It was really boring." BABS

Early birds: Michael Salter's 1997 portrayal of the superior Paxo, later dropped from the cast, who is flanked left and right by Babs and Edwina (who, in a different guise, now goes to the chopping block in the film).

This debate led to the devising of a story line that survived for some time, in which the chickens came from another place, a better farm, and finally ended up at Tweedy's Farm, which was like a prison camp. "We started with the chickens escaping from a nice, cosy little hill farm," explains Peter, "then we had them running amuck and causing all kinds of trouble. There was then an elaborate courtroom drama scene in which the farmer was charged with inability to care for chickens. The birds were taken away from the farmer (who was financially ruined), bundled into a police van and sent to this home for 'bad chickens' at Tweedy's Farm."

Eventually, there was a fourteen-page outline which included the bones of the present story together with a huge amount of other material that was to change or be lost over the next couple of years.

This outline was sent to Jake Eberts with a covering letter from executive producer Michael Rose in which he expressed the view that the idea had "developed substantially" and that Peter and Nick had "begun to find the key characters. I think it is sufficiently developed in their minds that a writer would assist now rather than blow them off track."

Color sketches by Michael Salter of Rocky addressing a line-up of characters as they were known in August 1997: Bunty (then a carrier pigeon); McNugget (later renamed Mac); Fowler; the abandoned Little Nobby; and Ginger.

Opposite, the cast, from Nick Park's sketchbook.

Hatching the Plot

In the first version of the story, dated August 1996 and headed by the single word "UNTITLED," Mr. Willard Tweedy is a strict vegetarian, although his wife, Melisha, occasionally craves a chicken dinner and raids the hen house. In the coop, Fowler is decidedly cock-of-the-walk, elderly and respected, but with an eccentric interest in bird-watching. Fowler's ambitious second-in-command, Haxby (in a story device that has parallels with George Orwell's *Animal Farm*), will eventually usurp Fowler's position and surround himself with loyal hench-chickens for protection.

Ginger, a rebellious and mischievous chicken, becomes infatuated with a desire to see the outside world after an encounter with Rocky, a wild chicken with "a dashing gypsy look about him," who refers to himself as "the Lone Free Ranger." Ignoring the advice of her friends Paxo and McNugget (named, respectively, after a British brand of poultry stuffing and a popular microwave-ready chicken dinner), Ginger escapes from the farm and goes in search of Rocky.

The story then becomes tangled. After various adventures, Ginger and Rocky embark on a life of crime together, their faces appearing on reward posters everywhere; a gag which recalls the wanted poster for Feathers McGraw in

The Wrong Trousers, showing the Penguin disguised as a rooster and the slogan, "Have You Seen this Chicken?"

Rocky abandons Ginger to her fate at the hands of the police and she is returned to Tweedy's Farm, which has now been transformed into a prison camp with high, barbed-wire fencing and lookout towers. Fowler has "been retired" and Haxby and his cronies are now running things along strict military lines. Despite the tightened security, it soon transpires that chickens are "going missing." Mr. Tweedy, suspecting the work of foxes, sends for a consignment of "Fox-B-Gone Robot Watch Dogs, the Farmer's Friend!," which clearly have associations with Preston, the cyber-dog, in *A Close Shave*.

At this point in the outline, it is possible to see the establishing of themes that, despite numerous changes, would eventually find their way into the finished film:

"Standing alone by the wire as autumn approaches, GINGER sees a flight of birds flying overhead. FOWLER appears beside her, and tells her that they're flying South. GINGER is angry, thinking of ROCKY.

"But FOWLER has something else in mind. GINGER realizes he's getting at

something. Then it hits her. Birds. . . . Flying South to freedom. She's a bird after all. . . . Perhaps . . ."

The plot hurtles wildly on. Rocky reappears. As conditions worsen, Ginger and her companions begin planning their escape. Under Fowler's supervision, they build a giant wooden albatross, covering the sounds of their labors with preparations for a "camp concert-party" that will feature a group called the Chicken Supremes.

Their escape almost succeeds. The albatross is launched and the Tweedys give pursuit: "MELISHA TWEEDY is really mad now. She climbs on to the back of the lorry and pulls off a tarpaulin to reveal an antiaircraft gun." A shell rips into the plane and "blows the flimsy Albatross to fragments." What will become of Ginger and the others?

"Chickens are scattered across the sky like confetti. They tumble down towards the dark waters of a lake below. It seems as if they are doomed, until GINGER shouts at them to flap, just flap. They're birds aren't they? One by one the chickens flap madly, their fall slows and eventually they're flying—more like bumble-bees than swallows—but at least they're aloft. . . . A squadron of chickens turns in the air and flies off into the sunrise."

Bunty   Babs

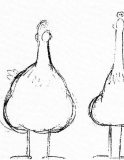
MRS. A. Average

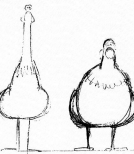
Mrs C Average

Mrs. D Average

Mrs. B. Average   Ginger   Rocky

Screenwriter Karey Kirkpatrick with Nick Park and Peter Lord during their story-planning trip to Yorkshire.

The man first chosen for the job was the British writer, Jack Rosenthal, who seemed an ideal choice, having a great comic sensibility and having worked in both television—with award-winning scripts for plays like the comedy-drama, *The Barmitzvah Boy*—as well as writing for the big screen on, among other films, Barbra Streisand's directorial debut, *Yentl* (1983).

Jack Rosenthal worked with Peter and Nick for some months, producing a draft script. The period was set as being the 1950s: a time when memories of the Second World War were still fresh in people's minds, but when there was also the hope and promise of the new Elizabethan era.

Fowler developed into a former flier with the Royal Air Force, vainly attempting to rule the roost with the faded authority of his former glory days.

Bunty entered the scene, not a chicken but a handbag-carrying pigeon (she was, of course, a *carrier* pigeon!) who had

once had a secret wartime romance with Fowler which was to have been shown in flashback sequences filmed in moody black-and-white photography recalling that classic British film romance of the 1940s, *Brief Encounter*.

Other characters came and went, but although the project had moved on, there was a growing feeling that the collaboration between writer and filmmakers wasn't working in the way everyone had hoped. Perhaps it was that Jack Rosenthal was used to writing solo and coming up with his own ideas rather than having to develop those of others. In the spring of 1997, with regrets on all sides, the decision was taken to look for another writer.

Jake Eberts recommended Karey Kirkpatrick, who had co-scripted *James and the Giant Peach*. Karey had several valuable skills: a former staff writer at Disney, he had co-written *The Rescuers Down Under* (1990) and worked on Disney's live-action comedy *Honey, We*

Shrunk Ourselves (1997). He was used to working in the collaborative way in which Hollywood screenwriters are traditionally required to operate. He understood comic timing and dramatic structuring and had a particular sympathy with writing for animation; he was, at the time, writing the script for *Thunderbirds*, a proposed feature-length live-action film based on Gerry Anderson's cult TV puppet series.

Karey knew of Aardman's work from the music video they had made for Peter Gabriel's "Sledgehammer" and from their talking Chevron car advertisements for American television. He had also seen *Creature Comforts*, *The Wrong Trousers*, and *A Close Shave* and was keen to work with the studio. There was, however, one serious obstacle to the collaboration: his native origins. There had been a strong feeling at Aardman that the project needed a British writer. This was something of which Karey Kirkpatrick was well aware when he flew from California to Bristol to meet with Nick and Peter.

Peter Lord's early sketch of the farm.

"They wanted a movie that would be very English," recalls Karey, who has perhaps a screenwriter's habit of rerunning past conversations: "We met and talked, and Nick said, right away, 'He gets it! I can work with him.' Pete, who likes to think about things, took a little longer to come round to the belief that I was the right man for the job. But once they had both agreed, it soon became clear that we were going to make a really good creative combination."

Karey was home in America when he got word that he was being commissioned to write *Chicken Run*. Not long after, he was once again on a plane heading back to England. During the flight and through the night in a London hotel, he completed his script for *Thunderbirds*, grabbed two hours sleep and set off by train with Peter and Nick for the dales of Yorkshire in the north of Britain which were to be the setting for the film.

An inspirational sketch by Roger Hall locates Tweedy's Farm within the wider setting of the surrounding countryside. Hall includes drystone walls typical of the Yorkshire Dales and depicts the way in which sun and cloud often mottle on the hills with light and shade.

Overleaf, a 1997 sketch by Michael Salter for Sunny Farm (later Tweedy's Farm) that establishes the appearance of a POW camp for chickens.

Magnus Pike Hen.

(mcNugget)

Nick

Various approaches to the character of McNugget (later Mac) from Nick Park's sketchbook, referred to here as the "Magnus Pike Hen," a joke on the name of a well-known bespectacled and eccentric scientist, Dr. Magnus Pyke, popular with British television audiences.

Study for McNugget by Michael Salter, August 1997

Study for McNugget by Polly Holland, October 1997

Rocky: Relax, we're making progress.

Arriving in Wensleydale (coincidentally the home of one of Wallace's favorite makes of cheese), writer and animators booked into a former royal hunting lodge (now converted into a bed and breakfast) and began grappling with the problems that divide field from field; village stores that sell anything and everything; and pubs filled with pipe smoke and the woody aroma of open fires. "One day," recalls Karey, "we had taken a walk and were sitting on a bench when suddenly

As Karey recalls, they came up with a lot of ideas while they were in Yorkshire: "Ideas that, for the most part, found their way into the finished film, which is a pretty rare thing to happen on an animated movie. I especially remember us thinking up this crazy scene in which Rocky is sitting in a hot tub giving flying instructions to the chickens, while some of the other birds are rubbing his back and one of them is blowing bubbles through a straw to make it like a Jacuzzi."

of shaping the story. The only givens were the basic facts of the story idea that had captured the imagination of Steven Spielberg and Jeffrey Katzenberg: it was going to be a POW escape movie with chickens and would end with the birds building a plane with which to "fly" to freedom.

"The three of us would meet every day," recalls Karey, "we'd try to pound out the story, but cracking a story is really not much fun, since it tends to come in fits and starts. Nick and Pete had never done it on a feature-length format and I think they were rather shocked at my way of working. Rather than sitting staring at one another, I look for diversion: 'Let's take a hike!' I'd say, or 'Let's go into town or take a look at that waterfall.'"

So, between whiles, they'd go for a walk on the hills, visit village pubs and market-places, and talk with local residents to give Karey a feel for the language. For the American, it was something of a crash course in a very specific aspect of British culture: little hamlets of mellow brick houses with grey-slated roofs, nestling in the folds of the hills; the drystone walls

dozens of sheep came hurtling past us with sheep dogs corralling them! I just *loved* the sheep dogs!"

Any doubts about engaging an American were soon forgotten in part because, as Karey puts it: "I came into this movie saying: 'This is your movie and I am your second lieutenant.'"

Peter Lord remembers how effortlessly Karey settled into a working relationship with himself and Nick: "What he did was enter into the project with a sensitive—almost withdrawn—attitude. He said: 'It's your film, I'm just here to realize it.' If he had come along, appearing to be the *auteur*, telling us what to do, I doubt if we'd have succeeded in working together. He was very clever in leaving any criticisms until we were comfortable with one another. It was only then that he started to say things like: 'I love these ideas, guys, but they really don't fit! You can't do it because you'll never get it all in the film.' By that time, of course, we were ready to listen."

One of the most significant changes Karey brought to the story was the making of

61

Study for Rocky by Michael Salter, December 1997.

Rocky into an American: "I thought if Ginger and Rocky's relationship was going to be somewhat cantankerous—rather like that of Katherine Hepburn and Spencer Tracy—then it might be interesting to bring in an element of culture clash: you have this brash, arrogant, cockerel—playing on the whole 'cocky' thing—and I thought it would work better if he were an American."

"Of course," laughs Peter Lord, looking back to those early story discussions, "as we've later joked with Karey, there was a sense in which *he* was the smooth-talking American who came in, confidently telling us that he was going to sort everything out."

Nick then had the idea that it might be funny if Rocky is going to teach the chickens how to fly and he were actually a circus rooster who had been shot out of a cannon. "That really made us laugh," says Karey, "so we thought: 'Well let's do that! Why not?' That's how major story points sometimes come about—almost by accident."

The idea of the expert who, in fact, knows nothing—and was American—was irresistible. Peter and Nick had recently attended a seminar on script structure, entitled "Know Your World," by the celebrated American scriptwriting guru, Robert McKee, and this provided Karey with a useful analogy to the Rocky situation: "I said, 'We're working on this movie and we're like all these chickens: we've got something that we have to do, the problem is working out exactly how to do it. Well, supposing, all of a sudden, Robert McKee just falls out of the sky—drops right into our chicken coop—and

starts telling us how to make the movie. And *then* we find out that this guy has never actually *made* a movie! How do we react? What do we do?' Thereafter, whenever we got stuck, one of us would say: 'OK, so Robert McKee falls into this room, right now, and . . .'"

Several other significant story developments were devised during the stay in Yorkshire, including the introduction of the pie machine, although the chickens were originally going to be taken away to another place in order to be put into the machine rather than, as in the film, having the machine delivered to Tweedy's farm.

The ideas flowed—and when they didn't, they just went for another walk to another pub until inspiration struck again—and the relationship developed into one of mutual trust and learning, perhaps not unlike the on-screen relationship between Rocky and Ginger. "I learned a lot from these guys," says Karey, "Nick is great with detail: he has an amazing mind for these little jewels of moments. And Pete is great with the overall story and the sensibility. In addition to which, he managed to beat out of me any tendency I might have had towards sentimentality. Americans also have a tendency to be a little more upfront with their feelings and, between them, they beat that out of me, too!"

At the end of June 1997, after two weeks in Yorkshire, the trio returned to Bristol with an outline. Then Karey Kirkpatrick flew home to California with four weeks in which to write the first draft of the script.

Making Rocky an American played on an old British wartime prejudice: "We often referred to that whole GI thing," says Nick. "The Americans coming in with all the money and their good looks—overpaid, oversexed and over here!"

"When you start writing an animated film, you have to remember that you are going to be working on it for three years, so you have to start very much like building a house. I lay the foundations, erect the framework, raise the walls, and maybe try to hang a few pictures and put a little furniture in there. Then I wait for other people's reactions. Whenever I get notes back on a draft, all I listen for is anyone attacking the framework. If

animation began. "As a result," remembers Karey, "we identified that it was all too long and needed some more work." Together with his wife and nine-month-old son, Karey moved to Bristol for a four month period of intensive work: "Day by day, sequence by sequence, page by page, I went over that script, cutting and trimming, tightening it up and getting it down to the right length."

Chicken Run shows a characteristically English aversion to excessive sentiment, especially in the character of Ginger, about whom Peter and Nick were in agreement. "They wanted a character who was really strong," says Karey. "The challenge was figuring out what her dramatic development was going to be in the story."

they're starting to talk about what I call the 'moveable pieces'—the furniture, the decorations—suggesting that maybe this line could be funnier or that character could be different, then that's fine. Just so long as what they're suggesting doesn't affect the structure, I know we're in pretty good shape."

In August, with the first draft written, Karey moved over to London, working on the *Thunderbirds* film during the week and travelling to Bristol every weekend to work with Nick and Peter on a second draft. This was followed by a third draft around Christmas 1997. By then the visualization process had begun at the studio with the creation of inspirational art in the form of designs for the chickens and the farmyard setting and various pictorial renderings of the story.

It was in the autumn of 1998 that Karey Kirkpatrick returned in company with Jeffrey Katzenberg and other DreamWorks executives. The plan was to have a final review of the story before

The decision was taken to consolidate some of the characters. A pair of "mute twins," called Sage and Onion, were among the first to be dropped, followed soon afterwards by Paxo who, from the beginning, had been established as one of Ginger's closest friends. Paxo was a champion egg layer and a solid, dependable workhorse, but in the streamlining process her role in the film passed to another chicken, Bunty.

Early drafts had also featured a chicken character called "Edwina" after Edwina Currie, a former junior health minister in Margaret Thatcher's Conservative government who, in 1988, made remarks about the safety of British eggs that triggered a crisis in the egg industry and brought about her resignation.

The name may have been a British "in-joke," but her personality was that of a universal type. As Karey Kirkpatrick puts it, "Edwina was a know-it-all-chicken; the poshest bird in the place; the final authority on all matters of decorum."

A crowd of characters from
Nick Park's sketchbook,
including the appealing
Nobby (upper left) as well as
the twins Sage and Onion and
the haughty Paxo. Below, the
last of Edwina in a storyboard
frame drawn by Don Lane.

"Nobby," recalls Karey Kirkpatrick, "was one of the first things that Jeffrey Katzenberg came after, believing that he changed the tone of the movie into something slightly younger and less sophisticated. At the time it was hard to let go, but I'm sure he was right."

Nick agrees: "It was a good decision. And you know, the odd thing is, you often feel liberated when you've finally let go of ideas that you've been desperately clinging on to."

The film went through a constant refining process: "One of the things I'm most proud of," says Karey, "is having kept the story small. And even though it's a very small movie and all the action takes place in one location, we've managed to keep it suspenseful and interesting: something is always happening in this small, contained space. Sometimes Peter and Nick would ask, 'Is this a big enough story point?' and I'd say, 'Let's make the *little*, BIG! Let's make big deals out of little things—a truck, a pie machine starting up—because it's what you guys do really well.'"

With the script more or less in shape—though it has continued to undergo revisions while animation has been in progress—two writers, Mark Burton and John O'Farrell, came on to the project to do some dialogue polishing. "They were terrific," says Karey, "not only did they check all my English, they came up with some very funny lines that are in the movie."

Once the film had gone into production, many further changes would take place, but the story was now established and in a shape not too different from that in which we now view it on the cinema screen.

However, it soon became clear that Edwina was going to have to go.

"At the time," says Karey, "the script called for a nondescript chicken who didn't lay enough eggs and, as a result, went to the chopping block. So one of us said: 'Well, since we've axed Edwina from the film, let's call *that* chicken Edwina.' Which is how the unfortunate Edwina got the chop—*twice!*"

Another casualty was Nobby, a young cockerel who looked up to Ginger and wore a sock on his head with a hole cut out for his face like a Balaclava helmet. A favorite of Nick's, Nobby had a pet caterpillar called Grubber who died but was then reborn as a butterfly, inspiring the chickens to build their flying machine.

A number of elaborate sequences featuring Rocky's time in the circus and his eventual escape from the world of the sawdust ring had to be deleted: in the end, the torn poster was all that remained of the circus. "That was an enormous decision to make," says Peter Lord, "the circus was a recurrent motif in the film, right to the end when the escaping chickens were going to fly right through the circus. Nobody said 'lose the circus,' it was just that scene by scene we came to acknowledge that we simply couldn't tell the story with true characters and keep every single scene we had originally planned."

"All that circus material," says Karey Kirkpatrick, "was eventually simplified into the torn circus poster and the idea that the chickens find out the truth about Rocky when they put the two pieces of that poster together and discover that the only reason he can fly is because he got shot out of a cannon. I particularly liked the symbolism of the picture that isn't what it appears to be."

First Flight

The first attempt at storyboarding the whole film was drawn by Martin Asbury working with Nick, Pete, and Michael Salter in 1997. As shown here, the story differs in many particulars from the finished film: the opening montage of escape attempts has not yet been developed; there are various characters present (such as Paxo, Sage, and Onion, and Nobby) who were later cut from the story; there is a different explanation for Rocky's "flying entrance"; Fowler has a taste for drink; Ginger discovers what happens to chickens at a separate processing plant and learns the truth about Rocky from a pigeon; the inspiration for the chickens' eventual escape comes from the metamorphosis of Nobby's caterpillar, Grubber, into a butterfly; and the climactic chase involves a complex sequence with a combine harvester. The text under each frame repeats the hand-written notes on the storyboard.

66

EXT. COOP
INTRO TO FARM CAMP

CHICKEN ESCAPES

CORNERED BY TWEEDY AND DOGS

MEET MRS. TWEEDY,
CHICKEN TAKEN AWAY

EXT. FARM WINDOW
SILHOUETTE THRU WINDOW, MRS.
TWEEDY DESPATCHES CHICKEN

CHICKEN COOP
WE MEET GINGER

CHICKEN COOP
NEXT DAY MEET FOWLER

MEET PAXO

EXT. FARM HOUSE
YAWNING TWEEDY EXITS

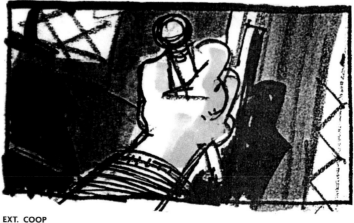

EXT. COOP
PULLS LEVER WHICH RELEASES

CHICKEN COOP
GRAIN INTO TROUGHS FROM SACKS?
FROM PIPES?

INT. HUT 7
THEY CAN'T GET DOOR OPEN

INT. HUT 7
WE MEET MCNUGGET AND MUTE
TWINS "SAGE" & "ONION"

CHICKEN COOP
CHICKENS POUR OUT OF HUT

HENS SEE CATERPILLAR

HENS PECK AT IT FROM ABOVE

MCNUGGET PUZZLES OVER DOOR WITH GINGER
NOBBY APPROACHES

GINGER STANDS UP FOR NOBBY

GINGER RUNS AROUND WITH
NOBBY "FLYING"

FOWLER'S HUT
FOWLER HINTS AT "MAY DAY" STORM

WILLARD OUTSIDE LINING UP HIS
DOGS

MRS. TWEEDY ORDERS "HEAD COUNT"

CHICKEN COOP
DOGS CHASE AND ROUND UP
CHICKENS

ON PARADE FOR HEAD COUNT

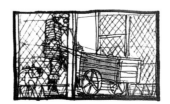

EXT. CHICKEN COOP
TWEEDY ENTERS WITH EGG CART

WE MEET THE TWO SCROUNGERS

NOBBY CALLS TO GINGER THAT HE'S
GOING TO FLY!

COOP TO DALES
GINGER ON ROOF
SEES THE DALES—SEES FREEDOM

CHICKEN COOP
GINGER TELLS EVERYONE—
NO ONE INTERESTED

EXT. CIRCUS
ROCKY ESCAPES FROM CIRCUS
GETS LIFT IN SIDE CAR

EXT. WOODS
MOTORBIKE COMBINATION
CRASHES—ROCKY FLIES OUT

EXT. COOP
ROCKY FLIES INTO COMPOUND
BOUNCES OFF ROOF ETC.

INT. CHICKEN COOP
CHICKENS POUR OUT OF HUTS TO
FIND OUT WHAT'S GOING ON . . .

GINGER MEETS ROCKY

BIG DIALOGUE—PAXO WANTS ROCKY
(WHO IS TRYING TO HIDE) TO BE THEIR
NEW COCKEREL

DRUNKEN FOWLER RELEGATED TO
SMALL HUT IN CORNER OF COOP

CHICKEN COOP HUTS
ROCKY ANNOUNCES THE NEXT
MORNING

HOCKEY GAME

HOCKEY GAME (LOADS OF GAGS?)

BELL RINGS

CHICKENS SCATTER BACK TO HUTS
GINGER IS CARRIED AWAY . . .

GINGER ROUNDED UP WITH OTHER
CHICKENS
HERDED INTO TRUCK—TRUCK PULLS
AWAY . . .

INT. PROCESSING PLANT
TRUCK PULLS INTO PROCESSING
PLANT

INT. TRUCK
TWEEDY OPENS BACK OF TRUCK TO
UNLOAD CHICKENS

INT. PROCESSING PLANT
MELISHA PUTS GINGER ONTO CONVEYOR BELT

INT. WRAPPING MACHINE
GINGER DUCKS AND BOBS AVOIDING
MACHINERY

GINGER IS "STAMPED"

LOADING DOCK
GINGER LOOKS IN HORROR AT
PACKAGED CHICKENS!

LOADING DOCK
GINGER RECAPTURED
"THERE YOU ARE!"

CHICKEN EXT. COOP
GINGER RELEASED INTO COOP

GINGER TELLS OTHERS WHAT SHE
HAS SEEN

STIR-CRAZY CHICKEN FREAKS OUT,
GOES UNDER FENCE . . .

. . . IS DEVOURED BY DOGS!

INT. HUT
THEY DISCUSS ESCAPE–
MCNUGGET CALCULATES

INT. ROCKY'S HUT
ROCKY CAN'T PACK FAST ENOUGH . . .

EXT. COOP
ROCKY (IN B.G.) SEES CIRCUS MAN
SHOWING POSTER TO TWEEDY

INT. COOP
GINGER SEES POSTER BLOW AGAINST
FENCE, IS SHOCKED
TALKS TO ROCKY

"WE NEED YOU"
DEAL IS STRUCK

GINGER & ROCKY TELL CHICKENS
THE PLAN IS THAT THEY FLY OUT

CHICKEN COOP
MR. TWEEDY TRIES TO FIND ROCKY IN
MORNING LINE UP

LATER–ROCKY EXERCISES THE
CHICKENS

TWEEDY PUZZLES OVER THE CHICKENS PRACTICING

INT. FOWLER'S HUT
FOWLER MUTTERS IN HIS DRUNKEN SLEEP
GINGER STORMS OUT

COOP
FAILURE AS THEY ATTEMPT TO FLY

ABOVE COOP
BIRDS WATCHING AND LAUGHING

COOP
FLIGHT ATTEMPT WITH SUSPENDERS (BRACES)

**GINGER: TELL THEM THE TRUTH
ROCKY: TELL THEM WHAT THEY WANT TO HEAR**

FOWLER HUT
FOWLER'S STILL SORRY FOR HIMSELF
GINGER IS POSITIVE

INT. COOP
MONTAGE IN RAIN–OF CHICKENS EXERCISING, FAILING TO FLY, ETC.

TOP OF HUT & VIEW
ROCKY GOES UP TO GINGER'S SECRET SPOT

ANGLE PAST F.G. FARMHOUSE
THE TRUCK OF DOOM RETURNS

INT. HUT
CHICKENS DEPRESSED
DEFEATED RATS ENTER WITH RADIO

ROCKY TURNS IT ON–THE CHICKENS ARE FRIGHTENED BUT SOON CALM DOWN

BIG DANCE NUMBER!
GINGER WATCHES ROCKY WORK HIS MAGIC

ROCKY ASKS GINGER TO DANCE

BIG MOVIE MOMENT

70

INT. FOWLER'S HUT
GINGER GOES TO TUCK FOWLER IN—
"DON'T TELL ME YOU'RE FALLING FOR
THAT RASCAL!"

CHICKEN COOP
NEXT MORNING GINGER LEARNS FROM
PIGEON HOW ROCKY "FLEW"

INT. CIRCUS TENT
FLASHBACK
ROCKY THRUST INTO CANNON, ETC.

CHICKEN COOP YARD
GINGER CONFRONTS ROCKY

SHE BEGINS TO SOB
ROCKY LEAVES

ROCKY ESCAPES—HIDING IN EGG
BUCKET

EXT. ROAD
ROCKY ON THE ROAD AND ON A
TRACTOR

CHICKEN COOP
CHICKENS DEPRESSED
GINGER BLAMES HERSELF

71

NOBBY SHOWS GINGER
GRUBBER IS DEAD!

FUNERAL—NOBBY BURIES
GRUBBER IN MATCHBOX

BUTTERFLY OUT OF MATCHBOX

NOBBY: "NOW WHY CAN'T WE
DO THAT?"

GINGER DRAWS IN THE DIRT

INT./EXT FOWLER'S HUT
GINGER TRIES TO CONVINCE
FOWLER HE'S NEEDED

INT. PLANE COCKPIT
FOWLER'S STORM FLASHBACK

COOP
NEXT MORNING THE "NEW" FOWLER
DESTROYS THE STILL

START MONTAGE
MCNUGGET WITH BLUEPRINT

HAND TEARING PAGES OFF CALENDAR

FARMYARD COOP
MCNUGGET AND GINGER STUDY MRS. TWEEDY'S BICYCLE

INT. BARN
SCROUNGERS TAKE TWEEDY'S TOOLS
AS HE WORKS UNDER CAR

COOP
FOWLER COMES UPON GINGER LOOKING
OUT AT THE COUNTRYSIDE—LOOKING
FOR ROCKY . . .

INT. HUT
CHICKENS PULL UP FLOORBOARDS
SAW & HAMMER

INT. BARN
WE LEARN ABOUT TWEEDY'S PRIDE &
JOY—HIS MINI

INT. HUT
CHICKENS UNDO DOOR PULLEY
SYSTEMS

INT. HUT
ASSEMBLY LINE OF CHICKENS TYING
STRANDS OF HAY & STRAW INTO
TWINE

FARMYARD
GAG OF TWEEDY IN TRASH CAN
MRS. TWEEDY DISCOVERS HIM

72

INT. HUT
MORE SEWING, HAMMERING, ETC. ETC.

HAND PULLS MORE PAGES OFF
CALENDAR

INT. HUT
GINGER ENCOUNTERS PAXO

CUT TO STREET
MEANWHILE CHILD ON TRIKE CHASES
ROCKY

BARN
ROCKY ENDS UP IN BARN, MEETS
ALLURING BARNYARD HEN

EXT. BARN
ROCKY REALIZES HE LOVES GINGER,
STARTS BACK TO COOP ON BACK OF PIG

INT. HUT
GINGER GIVES HER "AGINCOURT"—
ST. CRISPINS' DAY SPEECH

COOP–EXERCISE YARD
MORNING LINE UP

TWEEDY COMPARES FOWLER WITH
POSTER OF ROCKY

EXT. FARMHOUSE BY STEPS
RATS (NOW FAT) CAN'T RELEASE EGG
CART WHEELS

COOP–EXERCISE YARD
LITTLE NOBBY AND PALS DISTRACT
DOGS WITH HOCKEY GAME

ROCKY RETURNS—
GINGER DELIGHTED

[NO TEXT]

TUG OF WAR FOR WHEEL–
BETWEEN GINGER & DOG

INT. COOP
TWEEDY ATTACKED BY CHICKENS AND
TIED UP

GINGER SEES

FARMYARD
MRS. TWEEDY CAPTURING ROCKY
"BINGO!"

COOP
GINGER TELLS FOWLER THAT HE IS IN
COMMAND
SHE'S GOING TO RESCUE ROCKY

CHICKENS PULL CORDS
COUNTER-WEIGHTS MOVE, ETC.

FOWLER IN COCKPIT RISES THROUGH
FRAME

ALBATROSS REVEALED

INT. ALBATROSS
EVERY CHICKEN STARTING TO PEDAL

INT. HOUSE CORNER CABINET
GINGER RESCUES ROCKY

COOP
THE ALBATROSS STARTS TO MOVE

MOVING ABOVE ALBATROSS–
MR. TWEEDY APPEARS IN B.G.

INT. ALBATROSS
THE CHICKENS PEDALLING FURIOUSLY

COOP
EX. LOW ANGLE
MR. TWEEDY'S LEGS ENTER FRAME
ALBATROSS IN B.G. TO CAMERA

TOP SHOOT COOP
MR. TWEEDY–ALBATROSS–AND DOGS

COOP
LOW ANGLE TRACKING WITH PLANE TO
B.G. MR. TWEEDY

ANGLE
HE GRABS THE WHEELS

MR. TWEEDY CRASHES DOWN
ONTO FENCE

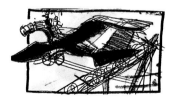

THE ALBATROSS FLIES!

DOGS TRAMPLE OVER TWEEDY

EXT. FARMHOUSE WINDOW
ROCKY AND GINGER CLIMB OUT
WINDOW. . . "IT WORKED!. . . IT'S FLYING!"

FARMYARD
MRS. TWEEDY BERATES MR. TWEEDY
AND SEES OUT OF THE CORNER OF
HER EYE

ROCKY AND GINGER RUNNING
INTO A BARN

LOW ANGLE
SECONDS LATER, THE MINI CRASHES
OUT OF THE BARN

INT. CAR
ROCKY STEERING–GINGER WORKING
THE PEDALS

EXT. LANE
CAR THRU FRAME–THE TWEEDYS
TAKE UP THE CHASE IN THE TRUCK

TOP SHOT
TWEEDY ENDS UP ON ROOF OF MINI. . .

GINGER AND ROCKY JUMP
FROM THE CAR . . .

TRUCK CRASHES INTO MINI–PUSH-
ING IT INTO THE COMBINE!

HOUSE DRIVEWAY
ROCKY & GINGER WATCH THE ALBA-
TROSS DIP OVER THE HILL

CHILD KNOCKED OFF TRICYCLE

OVER GARDENS
ROCKY AND GINGER SET OF ON TRIKE

HILL
THE COMBINE HARVESTER
CRESTS THE HILL

TRICYCLE STARTS TO JUMP THE FENCES
AND HEDGES–A LA STEVE MCQUEEN

THE COMBINE FOLLOWS–
CHEWING AND BALING EVERYTHING
IN ITS WAY . . .

THE CHASE CONTINUES THROUGH
ALL THE BACK-GARDENS

COUNTRYSIDE CLIFFTOP
CHASE CONTINUES UNTIL ROCKY
AND GINGER PEDAL OVER CLIFF

THEY FALL, TUMBLE THRU AIR

AND SUDDENLY THE ALBATROSS
SWOOPS IN UNDERNEATH THEM AND
THEY FALL INTO THE BELLY OF THE
WOODEN BIRD!

HARVESTER TO ALBATROSS
MRS. TWEEDY STANDING ON TOP OF COMBINE CLINGS TO THE WHEELS OF THE WOODEN BIRD

SHE THRUSTS HER HEAD THROUGH THE BOTTOM OF THE PLANE

INT. ALBATROSS
MRS. TWEEDY: "TURN THIS THING AROUND!" THE CHICKENS PECK HER

EXT. ALBATROSS
SHE LOSES HER GRIP AND FALLS!

WIDER OF THE SAME
FALLING OVER & OVER TO FINALLY . . .

MUDDY FIELD
. . . SHE CRASHES UP TO HER KNEES IN MUD!

C.U. MRS. TWEEDY:
"MR. TWEEDY! COME AND GET ME YOU WORTHLESS PILE OF PIG FILTH!" COMBINE APPROACHES IN B.G.

75

ANGLE ON COMBINE
MR. TWEEDY DRIVING THE COMBINE: "COMING, DUCKS!"

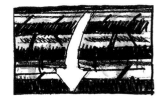

CLOSE ON THE WHIRLING BLADES—COMING TO CAMERA

MUDDY FIELD
COMBINE PASSES AND DISGORGES A BALE MADE UP OF MRS. TWEEDY

TWEEDY PACES IN FRONT OF BALE: "RIGHT, THERE'S GOING TO BE A FEW CHANGES AROUND HERE!"

ALBATROSS IN SKY
THE WOODEN BIRD STARTS TO SHED BITS—(IT'S BREAKING UP!)

INT. ALBATROSS
SUDDENLY—ALL THE COGS WHEELS PULLEYS AND WIRES—PING APART!

THE WHOLE OF THE PLANE SHATTERS TO PIECES—CHICKENS ARE TOSSED IN THE AIR AND THEY ALL START TO FALL!

EVERYONE TERRIFIED—ROCKY CALLS OUT: "THIS PART I DO KNOW! WINGS OUT EVERYONE!"

AND SUDDENLY THEY ALL ARE FLYING!

IN SILHOUETTE THEY FLY INTO THE SUN . . .

THEY LAND—EVERYONE CELEBRATES! GINGER AND ROCKY EMBRACE
THE BUTTERFLY LANDS ON NOBBY

PULL BACK FROM THEM AS THEY START TO DANCE "THE FUNKY CHICKEN!"

END OF BREAKDOWN

It all begins with the story, and you "read" the story on storyboards. The storyboard is, literally, a large board—or series of boards—onto which are pinned hundreds of sketches (some exquisitely drawn, others rough and impressionistic) that tell the story of the film in a pictorial form rather like the illustrations in a comic book.

The storyboard was first used at the Disney studio in the early years of sound pictures. Previously the sketches outlining a film had been scattered around on office floors or tacked onto walls so they could be viewed by the directors and animators. Then someone got the idea of pinning the sketches onto boards, which meant that the visual script for the film was suddenly portable and could be transported to script meetings or to the studios of the various animators who were working on the film. It also meant that the story could easily be changed: an individual drawing could be moved to somewhere else, thrown out, or substituted with another sketch altogether.

Although devised to aid the animation process, the storyboard was rapidly adopted throughout the movie industry. It was used to plan the scenes showing the burning of Atlanta in *Gone With the Wind* and is used today on all action and special effects movies.

Creating a storyboard can be, as Peter Lord explains, a consolidating process: "The visual script that makes up your storyboard is often bringing into focus all sorts of ideas that you may have been thinking about and working on for months, or even years!"

For Nick Park storyboarding a picture had always been a vital, and immensely satisfying, stage in the filmmaking process: "The storyboard," he says, "becomes the blueprint for the whole film and was always my chance to imagine it all, my opportunity to put my mark on it."

"I cannot work miracles cap'n. We're giving her all she's got." MAC

ROCKY: "Go! Go! Go!"

Chickens running and jumping off roof like paratroopers. Ginger the last to go, jumps, falls only inches.
PULL BACK to reveal a pile of chickens.

Overleaf: Ginger apparently doesn't believe that chickens can be taught to fly.

Storyboard artist Michael Salter is sitting at his drawing board, producing one of a great many drawings of chickens with flapping wings. "You have to use your imagination and try to think what it would be like to be a chicken," he says. Although his drawings will never actually be seen in the film, they will guide the animators who eventually create the scene with puppets.

81

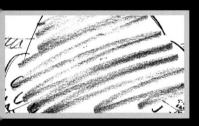

Storyboard artist Michael Salter (left) working with Nick Park on laying out storyboard sketches for Chicken Run

Screening rushes: the view from the perspective of projectionist Roger Sharland.

Indeed, during the early years at Aardman, the animators had always prepared their own storyboards. Nick had drawn all the sketches for *A Grand Day Out* and *The Wrong Trousers* and although studio artist Michael Salter had drawn the storyboard for *A Close Shave*, he worked closely from thumbnail sketches made by Nick. It was natural, therefore, that Nick and Peter would expect to draw the storyboard for their film.

It wasn't long before they realized that the storyboard was the first of many tasks that, on this occasion, they were going to have to share with others. Dream-Works had asked Aardman to prepare a story reel: a filmed version of the entire storyboard that could then be shown on a screen together with a full sound track of voices and a temporary music score.

This is standard procedure in animated feature filmmaking and has been followed—in some form or other—since the making of *Snow White and the Seven Dwarfs* in the 1930s. From his experience at both Disney and DreamWorks, Jeffrey Katzenberg was well aware that whilst it

The moment you see what it's going to look like, how the characters are going to relate to one another, how the gags will look, you instantly see what works and what doesn't.

might appear to be an unnecessary labor, the process can save time and money by allowing the film's dramatic and emotional structure to be seen—as it eventually will be seen—*on screen*.

"It is so telling," says line producer Carla Shelley. "The moment you whack it up on the screen and see what it's going to look like, how the characters are going to relate to one another, how the gags will play, you instantly see what works and what doesn't, where you have too much material and where there are great gaping holes. We soon saw that this was the only way to do it."

Before they could see what the story reel looked like when it was projected, there had to be a storyboard to photograph. Nick Park had made a number of preliminary sketches, establishing some of the key story moments, and Michael Salter began drawing up the storyboard. "The main difference," says Michael, "between what I did on *A Close Shave* and what I had to do on *Chicken Run* was that, instead of working up *drawings*, refining and polishing Nick's sketches, I was suddenly having to work up *ideas*—and hundreds of them!"

It was May 1998 and the story reel had to be completed by September. "It was," as Carla admits, "a naïve expectation on everybody's part that the storyboard could be drawn, filmed, and edited in three months. It soon became clear that it was going to take much longer."

A solution came from DreamWorks where a number of storyboard artists were on the staff, having worked on the studio's animation projects, including the computer-animated movie *Antz*, and the traditional animation feature *The Prince of Egypt*. DreamWorks offered the services of no less than fourteen storyboard artists for various sequences of *Chicken Run*.

For Peter and Nick this windfall presented a slightly alarming challenge: until now they had only been dealing with a relatively small group of "outsiders"—Jeffrey Katzenberg, Jake Eberts, DreamWorks producer Penney Finkelman Cox, and Karey Kirkpatrick—with all of whom they had established close relationships. Now they were going to have to tell—and in a way, *sell*—their story to a completely new—and unknown—group of people.

Flying to Hollywood, Peter and Nick pitched *Chicken Run* to the assembled storyboard artists and then spent three days working with individual artists whom DreamWorks had "cast" to illustrate specific sequences in terms of their particular specialities: romance, comedy, action sequences. In a fraction of the time that it would have taken Michael Salter—or even Michael and Nick working together—there was a finished storyboard. "Many of the drawings," recalls Carla, "were spot-on; a few were way off; while others offered new—even unexpected—takes on scenes and contributed visual gags and even added one or two lines of dialogue."

"For Nick and Pete," says story supervisor, Bridget Mazzey, "it was a great creative leap to go to the States, hand their story over to other artists and to then get all these pictures back."

To begin with the two men, who had already spent a great deal of time on *Chicken Run* and had very distinct ideas about how the film should look, had difficulty in "reading" the storyboard, particularly since it contained pictures in wildly

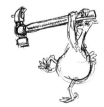

A "human figure" lumbers around from behind a hut. One of the dogs outside the fence sees it, nudges the other dog.

The figure trips and slams into the gate. The gate opens. The figure eases out until the back hem of the dress catches the fence. The dress slides off revealing . . . OUR CHICKENS, STANDING ON EACH OTHER'S SHOULDERS.

86

In one of their unsuccessful escape attempts, the chickens disguise themselves as Mrs. Tweedy. Here this idea is worked out in a sequence of drawings by Peter Lord and Michael Salter for eventual inclusion into the storyboard.

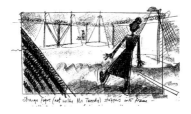

Strange figure (not unlike Mr Tweedy) staggers into frame

15

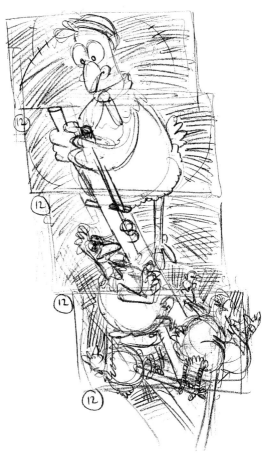

12

12

12

12

MR. TWEEDY: Oooh, What's all this, then?

MRS. TWEEDY: This is our future, Mr. Tweedy. No more wastin' time with petty egg collection and miniscule profits.

MR. TWEEDY: No more eggs? But . . . we've always been egg farmers. My father, and his father, and all their fathers, they was always . . .

MRS. TWEEDY: Poor! Worthless! Nothings! But all that's about to change. This will take Tweedy's out of the dark ages and into full—scale—automated— production. Melisha Tweedy will be poor no longer.

differing styles: from regular looking birds to ones with inordinately long necks or which looked more like Ninja Turtles than chickens!

"However," says Bridget, "once Pete and Nick had got used to that—and accepted the fact that the storyboard wasn't going to have the uniform, polished look they had imagined—I think they found it really quite exhilarating."

By October, when the Aardman and DreamWorks groups got together to review the story, the good news was that a completed story reel now existed on film. The bad news was that, as we have seen, it was too long. About twenty minutes had to be cut. While Karey Kirkpatrick revised the script, the action was also compressed.

A typical sequence to be revised was that featuring the arrival of the pie machine, which had originally comprised two separate scenes: one where the machine itself was delivered and another in which the Tweedys receive their supplies of peas and gravy. These were compressed into one scene, but only shortly before

the film was about to go into production. "Repeatedly," says Bridget, "we faced the realization that if we pulled or tweaked anything in the film, we ran the serious risk that we might affect something somewhere else."

That first "film" of *Chicken Run* that had involved everyone in such an agony of work and in so many uncertainties comprised a variety of roughish line drawings that, in flashing before the eyes, gave only the vaguest illusion of movement. But what it clearly did show was the strength of the story line and the characterizations that were reinforced by a soundtrack featuring a cast of the actors whose vocal performances would eventually become inseparable from the plasticine players for whom they spoke.

Opposite: In this close-up of Mrs. Tweedy embracing the pie machine, an animator's fingerprint is visible on her plasticine chin!

MRS. TWEEDY: Woman's touch. Makes the public feel more comfortable.

The chase through the interior of the pie machine is one of the most complex episodes in the movie. Shown on this page are storyboard drawings for this sequence by David Bowers that are continued on the next page with sketches by Nick Park, concluding with a final image by David Bowers. Notice how both artists convey not just the action taking place but also a highly energetic sense of movement and speed.

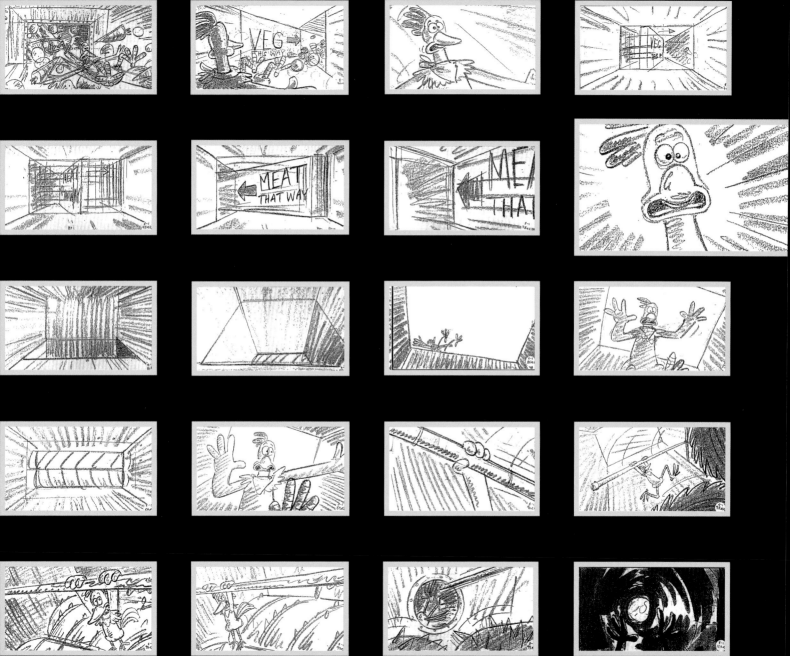

"Shall I do it again?" Red-headed Julia Sawalha, who is the voice of Ginger, is standing at a microphone with her script on a music stand. This is one of many recording sessions for the soundtrack of *Chicken Run*. At the moment they are taping Julia's dialogue for Scene 4200; and, yes, they would like her to do it again. This will be the ninth take.

The sound engineer confirms that they are recording and Julia runs the scene again, starting with Ginger's response to learning that Rocky is known as "The Lone Free Ranger." Screenwriter Karey Kirkpatrick—sitting in on the recording with Peter Lord, who is directing the actors—speaks Rocky's lines that will later be recorded by Mel Gibson.

GINGER: I knew it was possible.

Karey as **ROCKY**: Oh, it's possible all right.

GINGER: And I knew the answer would come.

Karey as **ROCKY**: Amen!

GINGER: We're all going to fly over that fence because Mr. Rhodes is going to show us how.

Karey as **ROCKY**: That's rrr . . . WHAT? Did you say *fly*?

GINGER: You can teach us.

Karey as **ROCKY**: Um . . . No, I can't.

According to the script: "Rocky hastily gathers his things. The chickens are shocked." So Kirkpatrick starts walking away from Sawalha. Later they will add what the script describes here as "Confused MURMURS," and Ginger will be seen holding up the "Flying Rooster" poster:

GINGER: This *is* you, isn't it?

"Don't worry. I'll teach you everything I know." ROCKY

Mel Gibson is the voice of Rocky

Julia has already had several attempts at saying the line, "a free chicken." She's said it various different ways: she's said it as if Ginger were relishing the concept of freedom and she's said it, stressing the word "free," to go with the move of pushing her way though the crowd of chickens surrounding Rocky.

Now she's starting to do variations on Ginger's puzzled inquiry, "This is you, isn't it?," as she looks from Rocky to the Flying Rooster poster and back again.

She tries, "This *is* you, isn't it?" Then, "This is *you*, isn't it?" And finally, "This is you, *isn't* it?"

There is a silence after the take. Peter Lord likes it. Julia winces and isn't so sure. "The trouble is," she explains, "I've said it so many times, it stops making any sense to me at all. Well, that's how I feel, any-way." She pauses and then—collapsing into laughter—adds, "And it's usually on the takes *you* like."

So—trying to keep all that in her head— Julia gets ready for take *ten*. Then, just before they record, there's a final piece of advice from the director: "Right then," says Peter Lord, "so the tone is about *accusation*. And like, *bigger*. Wide open."

They record the lines. There's another pause. Julia looks at Peter and bursts out laughing: "I *love* watching your face."

"No, no," says Peter, reassuringly, "I'm sure we've got it. . . ."

"You can't be sure," counters Julia, "you have *got* to be certain." And so they go for yet another take.

94

Anyone who supposes that recording the voices for an animated film is an easy task should attend one of these recording sessions and discover the truth: it is hard work. It requires an actor to be intensely focused, willing to have a go at just about anything, to do it over and over again till it sounds absolute twaddle, and not have much to go on apart from a few drawings.

That is how it has always been done in animation: first comes the script, then the storyboard, and then—before the animation begins—the voices are recorded. In the early years, dialogue was kept to a minimum, but once short cartoons had grown to feature length, it was inevitable that a lot more talking would have to go on. Everyone working on the film needs to understand the pacing and timing of the various scenes and those are, to a large extent, dictated by the vocal performances.

Once the animators have a voice track to work from, they can study the characters' inflexions and intonations and can calculate how to synchronize lip movements—or, in the case of the chickens in *Chicken Run*, "beak movements"—with the words that are being spoken.

At Aardman, whilst they have a lot of experience of marrying sound and image, they have not previously had to cope with a major soundtrack cast. Their early films used "vox pop" recordings of *real* people, then with the Wallace and Gromit films they had two central characters: one was a dog who didn't speak and the other a man who only had a handful of lines in each movie.

Nevertheless, the studio was well aware of the importance of vocal casting. The

Julia Sawalha is the voice of Ginger

performance by veteran British comic actor Peter Sallis, who provided Wallace's slow, deliberate, Northern tones, had contributed greatly to the character's popularity with audiences.

The first essential for an animated film voice is that it should be individual and contribute to our understanding of the character. Consider the worldly wise-cracking vocalizations created by veteran cartoon voice Mel Blanc for Bugs Bunny or the spluttering bad-tempered squawks which Clarence Nash gave to Donald Duck. The characters sound the way they look and move and—once heard—it is impossible to imagine them speaking in any other way.

GINGER: Which part of they kill us do you not understand?

ROCKY: Hey, I got my own set of problems to worry about.

ROCKY: Besides, this birdcage can't be that hard to bust out of. Watch me.

ROCKY: Couldn't agree more.

ROCKY: And I will be leaving—that way.

98

MIRANDA RICHARDSON (Mrs. Tweedy), who recently appeared as the despotic Queen of Hearts in a star-studded television version of *Alice in Wonderland*, has had few opportunities to play villains. She has worked for some of cinema's finest directors including Louis Malle, Robert Altman, Neil Jordan and Tim Burton as well as Steven Spielberg.

TONY HAYGARTH (Mr. Tweedy) has worked extensively in television and is a prolific National Theatre actor. His Shakespearean roles include Shylock, Macbeth, and Hamlet. He has also played Sancho Panza in *Don Quixote* and Vladimir in *Waiting for Godot*.

MEL GIBSON (Rocky) achieved international fame with the trilogy of *Mad Max* movies, which created his early screen persona of renegade and maverick. His reputation as an action hero (who could also play comedy) was reinforced by his *Lethal Weapon* films. Any tendency to typecast him as a performer has been countered by a variety of roles in different kinds of films, including *The Year of Living Dangerously*, the roistering historical drama *Braveheart*, and, most surprising, the lead in Franco Zefferelli's film of *Hamlet*.

JULIA SAWALHA (Ginger) is known to television viewers on both sides of the Atlantic for her portrayal of Saffron "Saffy" Monsoon in three series of the BBC's hit comedy *Absolutely Fabulous*. Her film credits include Kenneth Branagh's *In the Bleak Midwinter* and leading roles in television productions of *Pride and Prejudice* and *Martin Chuzzlewit*.

JANE HORROCKS (Babs) was widely acclaimed—both on stage and film—for her playing of the eponymous heroine of *The Rise and Fall of Little Voice*. Among her other credits are a diversity of stage roles (from Lady Macbeth to Sally Bowles in *Cabaret*) and film appearances in Mike Leigh's *Life Is Sweet*, Nick Roeg's *Witches*, and Michael Caton-Jones's *Memphis Belle*.

IMELDA STAUNTON (Bunty) played the Nurse in *Shakespeare in Love* and, in an appropriately Shakespearean vein, has also appeared in Trevor Nunn's film of *Twelfth Night* and Kenneth Branagh's film of *Much Ado About Nothing*, while her stage career has included leading roles in *The Beggar's Opera*, *Guys and Dolls*, and *The Wizard Of Oz*.

LYNN FERGUSON (Mac) is a writer, actress and stand-up comic, who has performed in revues, satires and pantomimes on both sides of the Scotland–England border.

BENJAMIN WHITROW (Fowler) has had a distinguished career acting with, among others, the National Theatre and the Royal Shakespeare Company. He has acted in plays by Ibsen and Chekov, been directed by Jonathan Miller and Harold Pinter, and portrayed some of the great Shakespearean comic roles from Falstaff to Malvolio.

TIMOTHY SPALL (Nick) is best known for his performance as Morris in Mike Leigh's *Secrets and Lies*. In a prolific career, Timothy has worked extensively on stage, television, and film, for Bernardo Bertolucci on *The Sheltering Sky* and for Kenneth Branagh on both *Hamlet* and *Love's Labours Lost*.

PHIL DANIELS (Fetcher) is a veteran of the Royal Shakespeare Company whose work there ranges from *The Merchant of Venice* to *A Clockwork Orange* and whose many television credits include adaptations of Charles Dickens, situation comedies and modern dramas from the controversial *Scum* to *Sex, Chips and Rock 'n' Roll*.

FOWLER: I don't like the look of this one. His eyes are too close together.... And he's a Yank.

ROCKY: Easy pops. Cockfighting is illegal where I come from!

BUNTY: And where is that exactly?

ROCKY: Just a little place I call the land of the free and the home of the brave.

MAC: Scotland!

ROCKY: No—America.

FOWLER: Poppycock! Pushy Americans, always showing up late for every war. Overpaid, oversexed, and over here!

Opposite: Fowler greets the day. To achieve the necessary spatial perspective behind him, Fowler is filmed standing on a dummy roof positioned in front of the set and supported by rigging, which will not appear in the finished film, of course.

British actor Benjamin Whitrow is standing in front of a microphone going: "Cock-a-doodle-doo!"

Whitrow is recording his lines as Fowler. He crows in exactly the kind of way you would expect from Fowler: a clipped, Royal Air Force–type crow. He does it several times and then adds an inspired touch—one of those upper-class vocal ticks such as Terry-Thomas might have used in British comedies of the 1950s. This time it comes out as, "Cock-a-doodle-doo, what what?!"

Everyone applauds. Benjamin smiles and murmurs modestly: "Of course, they'll all think it's Nigel Hawthorne."

It is often remarked that there are parallels between acting for animation and acting on radio—and indeed some of the best voiceover artists are those who have mastered the discipline of radio, where everything about a character has to be conveyed in the vocal performance.

Nevertheless, given the chance, there is always a tendency to "act scenes out," even if there aren't any costumes or settings. At one of the *Chicken Run* recording sessions, Whitrow as Fowler is joined by fellow chickens Imelda Staunton as Bunty and Lynn Ferguson as Mac.

Watched by Sawalha (who is desperately trying not to giggle) they play out an early version of a scene where Ginger finally gives into the gloomy realization that they are all doomed and Fowler starts nattering on about not giving in to defeatist attitudes and about his beloved flying badge.

Suddenly, Bunty shouts at Fowler, "Will you shut up about your stupid, bloomin' medals?" She knocks it out of his hand, he retaliates, Mac joins in, and suddenly three grown-up people are sparring about, screeching and squawking like angry birds. It is obvious that they are not only having fun, but are entering into the business of *being* their characters—even if those characters are chickens.

Because the voices must be recorded before beginning the animation process, the voice talents have the opportunity to make their own contribution. Here Staunton does several additional, different, takes on her Bunty line to Fowler about his badge in order to give the directors a range of interpretations from shouted anger to dismissive tiredness.

It also allows for occasional ad-libbing, which may, or may not, make it into the finished film, but which may give a refreshingly new slant on characters that

FOWLER: Company!—Cock-a-doodle-doooo, what what!?

Storyboard frames by
David Bowers.

ROCKY: Flying takes
three things. Hard work.
Perseverance. And . . .
hard work.

FOWLER: You said
hard work twice!

ROCKY: That's because it
takes twice as much work
as perseverance.

the director has probably already begun to take for granted.

Nick and Fetcher, the two opportunist rats, are played respectively by Timothy Spall and Phil Daniels. At yet another session, the two men face each other across the studio: Tim, as the bossy, argumentative, know-it-all Nick, wears a striped T-shirt and sits on a stool. Phil, the anxious, put-upon, slightly less bright Fetcher, stands adjusting his spectacles with characteristic nervousness. They are having a conversation that is currently scheduled to run over the film's closing credits, about which came first, the chicken or the egg.

As they do take after take they add a line here, a word there, turning a scripted joke into a piece of living conversation: it's all right for Fetcher to say you need an egg in order to get a chicken, but surely—before that—you need a chicken to lay the egg from which you get the chicken to lay the egg. . . .

The process is organic: the characters become an amalgam of Nick and Peter's sketches and the lines they have been given to say, together with something of the personality of the actors who lend them their voices.

Many animated features use stars both to ensure strong vocal performances and to enhance interest in the films. It is a tradition as old as the animated feature. From the mid-forties onwards, animated films increasingly featured the voices of movie stars such as Bing Crosby, Basil Rathbone and Boris Karloff. The leading character in DreamWorks' *Antz* was voiced by Woody Allen and *The Prince of Egypt*

had an all-star cast including Val Kilmer, Ralph Fiennes, Michelle Pfieffer, Sandra Bullock, and Steve Martin. If the initial decision to make Rocky an American rooster was inspired, then so, too, is the voice casting of Mel Gibson. No stranger to the business of speaking for animated characters (he was the voice of John Smith in Disney's *Pocahontas*), Mel brings his own dimension to the character of Rocky. When the rooster gives a hen-house lecture on the art of flying, the chickens (with the one exception of Ginger) are enthralled and impressed:

"So. You wanna fly, huh?. . . Well it ain't gonna be easy. And it ain't gonna happen overnight, either. . . . Flying takes three things. Hard work. Perseverance. And . . . hard work." Mel perfectly captures the smooth, effortless charm of the experienced bluffer; the laid-back, cocky American ease of a character who fails to see that if he wants to win over a highly independent chicken like Ginger, calling her "doll face" may *not* be the way to do it.

Sometimes, animated features incorporate caricatures of the voice talents' features into the character designs. So the Mad Hatter in *Alice in Wonderland* looked exactly like veteran comic Ed Wynn, and Shere Khan in *The Jungle Book* was the very personification of George Sanders, who provided the tiger's sneering voice.

At Aardman there is no attempt to give the animated characters any of the aspects of their vocal counterparts. The gaunt and intimidating Mrs Tweedy, for example, looks nothing like Miranda Richardson.

Describing her screen character, Richardson says: "She is relentless and rules with a rod of iron. She is vile to Mr. Tweedy; vile to the chickens; vile full-stop! She is thin and crabbed and pinched by her existence, but she has a vision that life can be different somehow."

Richardson has been called back to record some retakes. Seated in front of her script in the recording studio, she chats with Peter Lord. Her voice is soft and carefully modulated and there is a thoughtfulness in the way in which she chooses her words.

Someone is reading Mr. Tweedy's lines in the absence of Tony Haygarth, who plays Miranda's slow-witted, hen-pecked husband. The scene is 12300, in which the Tweedys discover that the chickens have flown the coop. According to the script, "Mrs. Tweedy is freaking out."

The recording begins and Miranda—whilst still managing to look calm and collected—suddenly bursts into the Northern, nutmeg-grater voice she has created for Mrs. Tweedy, spitting out words that will eventually be dropped from the movie with pure venom: "What *happened*? What have you *done*?"

Mr. Tweedy can only stammer in reply, "Th . . . th . . . they've escaped!"

Again Mrs. Tweedy explodes: "To the car! They're getting away. OUR PROFITS ARE GETTING AWAY!!"

Reflecting on providing a voice that will, eventually, emerge from a lump of plasticine, Richardson betrays an anxiety about the process: "It's odd, because

you're not sure what value your contribution has. When you've recorded everything, a version will be picked that works for the best, but you can't see it happening."

To Guionne Leroy, one of the film's key animators, there is no question about the importance of the vocal recordings: "The voice is what guides us. It's absolutely crucial in bringing the animation alive. The first step is always to listen to the voice because the character is already in that voice. Our job as animators is to capture the energy in the voice and translate it into movement."

But in order to be able to move, the voices need bodies, and those bodies—whether for human beings or chickens—have also to be created. . . .

MRS. TWEEDY: Get the chickens.

103

"We needed a character who could easily get in and out of the chicken run," says Karey Kirkpatrick. "Since rats are known as being scavengers and scroungers I suggested we use a couple of rat characters. I came up with the names 'Nick' and 'Fetcher,' although it took a long time for Nick to agree to having a character with his own name appearing in the film."

"The trouble is, the animators will keep stealing it!" Jan Sanger, model production designer, is pointing at a board to which are attached plastic bags containing sample lumps of different colored plasticine, arranged according to the characters in *Chicken Run* and their body parts: "Head," "Beak," "Wing," "Eyelids," etc. "This was intended as a reference guide, but whenever the animators run out of plasticine for a character's eyebrows or something, they come in and raid these bags."

If you walk around Aardman Animation's studios, where *Chicken Run* is actually being shot, it comes as something of a surprise to discover that the most apparent difference between this and a conventional studio is one of scale. The tasks that need to be done to prepare for a live-action picture—designing and building sets, making props and costumes—have also to be done here, only the results are in miniature. All the same skilled people are in evidence: carpenters, electricians, gaffers, cameramen, special effects technicians, floor managers, and continuity persons. There is, however, one significant difference, in that—in addition to sets and props—here they also have to make the *actors*!

Shown into a storeroom in the model-making department, I find myself surrounded by shelves littered with pieces of chicken. It is a kind of comic-strip abattoir: feet with no bodies, headless torsos and beakless heads. There are boxes of tiny eyeballs (small beads, the holes of which are used to swivel the eyes in their sockets) and lots of sets of miniature teeth. At Aardman, the old adage "as rare as hens' teeth" couldn't be further from the truth.

"It's all in me head, it's all in me head . . ." MR. TWEEDY

Model maker Diane Holness and multiples model maker Jemma Proctor in the model-making shop: Aardman is an unusual studio in that the actors have to be made!

106

Right, design team supervisor Kate Anderson puts the finishing touches on the final sculpt of Fetcher; far right, sculptor Lisa Newport works on the very first prototype for an average chicken. Below, chicken eyes in the course of being painted.

Armature designer Andrew Bloxham rigs Ginger's legs to a bouncing pie.

Above, left to right: design team leader Claire Drewett works on an early prototype of Rocky; senior costume designer Sally Taylor makes a dress pattern for Mrs. Tweedy; deputy puppet production designer Anne King puts the finishing touches on a final sculpt of Mr. Tweedy. Left, a mold for a beak.

"We're still turning out three or four chickens a week," says Jan Sanger. "It's a constant conveyor. We just need to keep making chickens. We'll have to make chickens for the scenes inside the crate. Those might all be special chickens, because they've all got to sit on bicycles. And we're still building birds for the pie sequences. Rocky and Ginger landing on pies, Rocky and Ginger getting covered in gravy. We're into a big pie-veg mode at the moment."

Jan picks up the bulky body of a Bunty puppet and upends it to reveal the chicken's ample rump, which at the beginning of the film prevents her from successfully getting under the wire of Tweedy's farm. Bunty's rear is covered in a mass of little feathery shapes. "How many fluffles," Jan asks, "do you think there are on Bunty's bottom?" Frankly, it's difficult to guess and impossible to count.

"Fluffles," it turns out, is one of those words that means nothing outside the Aardman studio—and Jan Sanger's home. It was coined by Jan's young son, who, impressed by the hairs on his father's legs, inspected his own legs and gleefully announced, "Look, Mum, I've got fluffles growing on *my* legs, too!" Fluffles seemed a suitable word for the little semicircular bumps that cover the feather-petticoats worn by the chickens. Bunty, it turns out, has 3,077.

I can't help wondering whether they had considered feathers. "No!" says Jan, firmly. "Never! If we had put feathers on the bodies, then we'd have had to put them on the wings—and you couldn't have covered the wings in feathers because they're made of plasticine and it would have made them impossible to animate." The model-making department is where character design concepts are tested against the practical demands of the animators.

Each puppet created for animation has one thing in common with a real body, it requires a skeleton to hold everything together and to enable the figure to move. In animation, this skeleton is called an "armature" and can be made, at its simplest, from twisted wire or, as with the birds in *Chicken Run*, from meticulously

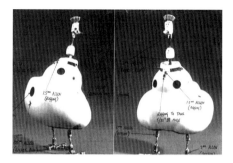

The anatomy of a star: the first of the chicken characters to be made into a puppet was Bunty. On this and the following pages, we see Bunty's evolution into fully animated life. Top and opposite, photographs and blueprints show Bunty's steel armature, the "skeleton" that allows her to be animated. The head of the armature has places to locate the eyes and the beak and the body has various "rigging" points where rods can be attached to support the figure when running or flying. Above, painter Arlene Arrell is touching up an "average B" chicken, whose form is similar to Bunty's.

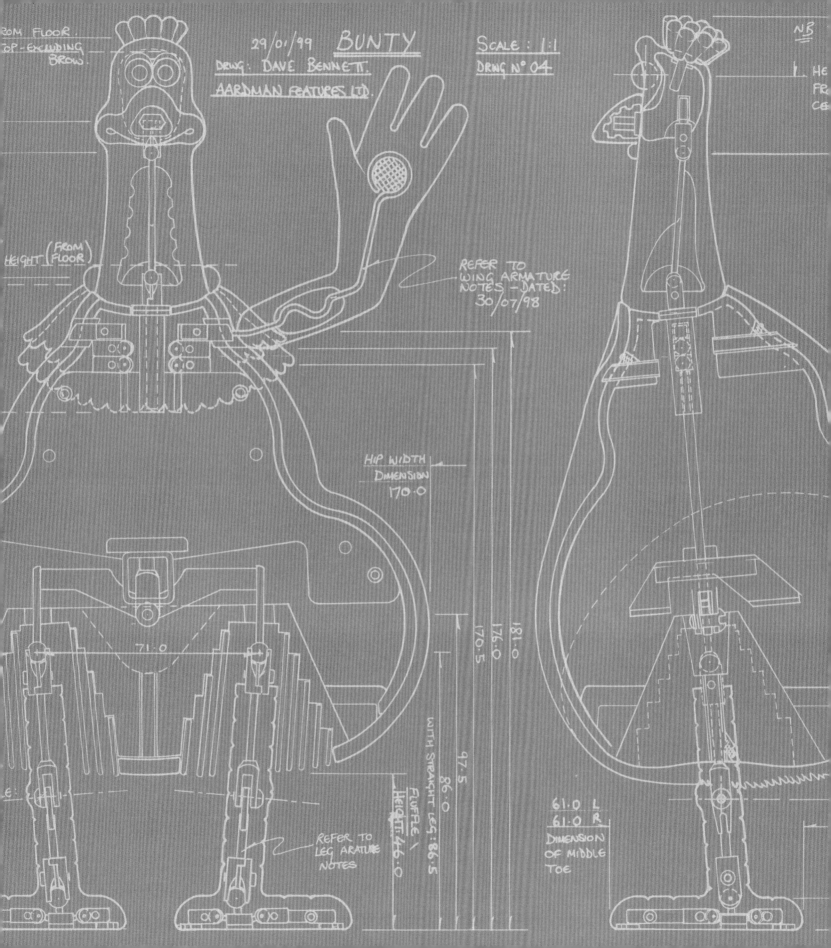

Right, early Bunty proto-type, 1997. Below, sculptor Linda Langley is sculpting the original Bunty prior to making molds.

milled rod-and-joint constructions that allow for maximum subtlety of movement. The armature supports the weight of the puppet and holds it rigidly in position while it is photographed, repositioned, and re-photographed to a total of twenty-four times for every second of film.

This armature skeleton is then "fleshed over" with whatever material the filmmaker is using—which, in the case of the Wallace and Gromit films, was plasticine. But plasticine produces puppets that are not durable, requiring that many be made over the course of a film, and no practical armature was going to hold the weight of plasticine chickens as Nick envisioned them. Perhaps only the most obsessive follower of Aardman will be shocked to hear this, but it required a real change in the studio's folkways to forsake this comfortingly familiar modeling material.

"When we were making *A Close Shave*," recalls supervising animator Loyd Price, "every Gromit used to be built by hand. It took a really experienced model-maker a day to build a Gromit and that's just too slow, especially when you are making a film that has ten main characters, plus hundreds of extras." Those numbers can be multiplied by however many of the studio's twenty to thirty animation units are filming at any one time since, unlike a live actor, one of the players in *Chicken Run* might be filming ten or more different scenes simultaneously. And each model of a particular character must be absolutely identical. At the time I am talking with Jan, there are no fewer than fifteen "Gingers" and twelve "Rockys" either filming on the sets or

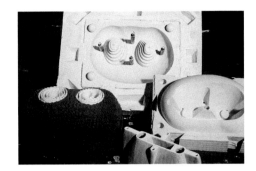

For every part of every chicken there exists a mold from which additional models can be cast as required.

Model making is meticulous and precise work. Arlene Arrell is press-molding a chicken "wing-hand" made by lining two sides of a mold with plasticine between which is embedded a wire skeleton providing the "finger bones" that will enable the animator to create convincing hand movements.

Top row: molds for casting Bunty's body showing the "fluffle-cups," the layered frills of feathers that conceal the point at which the legs fit onto the armature. Second row, left to right: the molds for Bunty's head, which will be made of plasticine; a mold for producing Bunty's comb; and a mold for making one of Bunty's beaks which will fit onto a location point in the skull.

Multiples model maker Claudia Hecht sands fluffles, above, and works on the skin that covers a puppet's armature, right.

Multiples model maker Michael Hares sticks under-arm fluffles on Buttercup, an "average B" chicken.

The realization that the use of plasticine would be impractical for the chickens of *Chicken Run* led to wider discussions about the degree of realism they were aiming to achieve. Nick, however, was adamant about what he wanted: "These chickens are stylized and that is how we're going to make them. We will work within that design."

Opposite: Chickens show their fluffles! Bunty is caught under the fence. The unfinished edge of the set is visible at lower left.

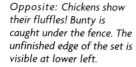

Opposite: Bunty leads a crowd of running chickens. Even though the puppets can stand on their own, they must frequently also be supported by rigging, which has to be retouched out of scenes where it is visible.

resting in the model store. "In any shot," she says, "every feather of every chicken *might* be seen. They all have to be made to the same exacting standard."

Which is why Jan was clear about how the chickens were—or were *not*—going to be made: "Well, I knew it wasn't going to be done with plasticine. Nick, Pete, and I spent some time at the end of 1996 playing with white plasticine, making chickens. It was a little bit like a therapy class, really. We tried to understand what our limitations were going to be: basically, these characters are chickens and—the way Nick drew them—they looked a bit like footballs walking around on long thin legs. Everyone could see that it just wouldn't work with the weight of all that

plasticine piled onto those spindly little legs." On top of which, Loyd Price adds, "We would have needed three times the number of people just to keep plasticine puppets clean." (The soiled surface of a plasticine puppet needs to be scraped away and replaced with fresh material.)

In *Chicken Run*, the bodies of Rocky, Ginger and the others are, in fact, made of silicon that has been cast from rubber molds taken from sculpted figures that are prototypes for each character. With silicon each chicken weighs in at rather less than half what it would have weighed if it had been made out of plasticine, and silicon matches well with the look of plasticine, retaining its hand-crafted look—including a few modelers' finger marks—whilst making a figure that is durable and infinitely renewable. There are no cleanliness problems with silicon chickens. "You just wash them over with a baby-wipe," explains Jan, "and you don't lose any of the detail or decoration, such as the hand-painted highlights on the chickens' fluffles." Apart from their ability to withstand days, weeks and months of handling ("We haven't re-skinned some of the chickens for a year," enthuses Jan), the silicon bodies have eased the need to have people constantly remaking puppets from scratch.

Still, the chickens required wings, heads, and, in some cases, legs of plasticine, since these must be animated, and silicon is not flexible. The studio had some experience working with a combination of plasticine and solid units in its previous shorts and TV commercials. The birds in *Chicken Run* are similarly constructed, which is why the chickens wear scarves: to conceal the point at which the heads join the necks.

"The standard chicken in Chicken Run couldn't even reach the ground in order to peck the dirt!" Harry Linden points out. "It is actually incapable of doing what a real chicken would do!"

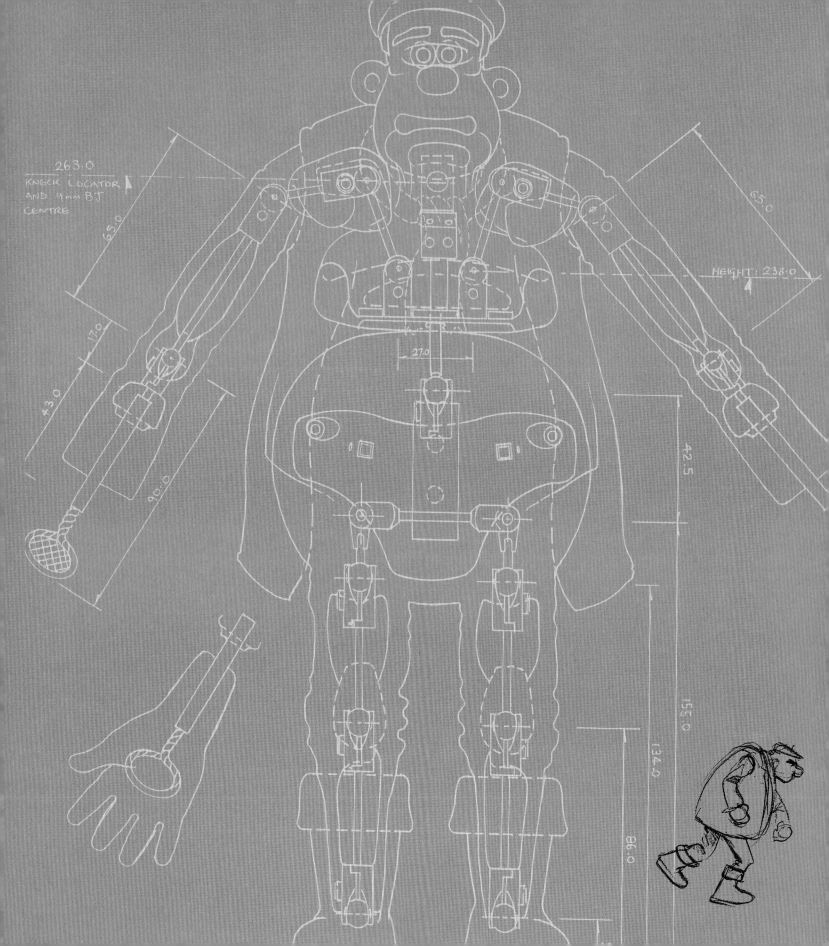

263.0
KNECK LOCATOR
AND 9mm BJ
CENTRE

65.0

17.0

43.0

90.0

65.0

HEIGHT: 238.0

27.0

42.5

155.0

134.0

86.0

Here, key animator Suzy Fagan works on a scene in which only Mr. Tweedy's legs and boots appear, so it is sufficient to use a puppet finished from the waist down. Because of the disparity in scales between chickens and humans, many puppets are built to two scales. A large Mr. Tweedy puppet is used for scenes like this one where he appears with the twelve-inch-tall chickens. (In other scenes, the standard twelve-inch-tall Tweedy puppets are paired with two-inch-tall chickens.)

Many stages are involved in bringing an animated character to life. At the beginning of the design process, animator Darren Robbie is photographed for reference in costume as Mr. Tweedy.

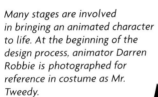

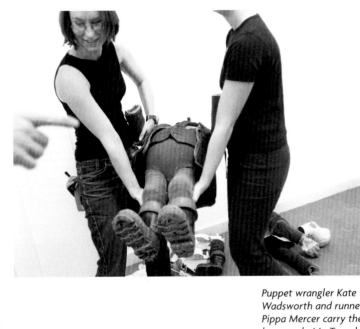

Puppet wrangler Kate Wadsworth and runner Pippa Mercer carry the large-scale Mr. Tweedy.

Armatures for Mr. Tweedy's feet.

"There was a lot of debate about the scarves." recalls Jan. "We had been trying to devise a way of hiding the seam between the head and the body. Eventually we came up with a stylistic approach: the chickens all wear scarves or necklaces or some accessory or other that would disguise the join. It took ages for everyone to actually buy into the idea of scarves. But once they had accepted that these chickens wear scarves, it ceased to be a problem."

For speed and uniformity, the plasticine wings and heads are all press-molded over a small wire bone-structure. This means that these parts can easily be replaced or remolded as they get "trashed": the all-purpose term covering wear and tear ("wings we go through a lot of . . .") as well as the grubbiness that results from so much handling and manipulation. Indeed, there are two people who spend each and every day press-molding new wings and beaks and who—at around halfway through production—have used no less than 3,370 pounds of plasticine!

"For the animator," says Loyd Price, "having these pieces pre-molded means that you can still 'tweak' the models, but you know the sculpture is already 90 percent

there. So, it's a bit like Morgan making cars: it's hand finishing rather than hand building."

Although made of plasticine, the chicken heads all have replaceable beak units that can be located onto face shapes that don't actually have anything much below eye-level. By changing beaks (or, in the case of the Tweedys, mouths), different facial expressions can be created and lips and beaks can be synchronized with the dialogue.

Inside each plasticine head-piece is a solid unit—a "beak locator"—to which the various beaks are fitted. As Jan Sanger explains, "Beak locators are vital. Without them, the beaks would look as if they were drifting around on the faces. It's easier with Mr. and Mrs. Tweedy because they have human faces and, because the mouthpieces are the same flesh color, they can be blended into the face. But chicken beaks are much harder because they just sit on the front of the head and it's absolutely crucial that they are located in the right place—and then *stay there.*"

In *Chicken Run* there may be as many as twenty characters in a scene, all of whom are speaking, making sounds, or giving

facial responses. Synchronizing speech is a skill that Nick and Peter have been perfecting on film since Aardman's *Lip Synch* series, but never on such a vast and complex scale.

The process of making a chicken seem to speak begins with a series of mouth and beak shapes that correspond to various letters or sounds. Once approved by the directors, model making breaks them down into component parts—top and bottom, beak and teeth—and makes molds of the shapes so parts can be cast.

Things aren't much simpler when it comes to the humans. For example, Mr. Tweedy has a series of replacement plasticine mouths that fit onto his face under the nose. His hair is made as a solid piece that slides into place, while his eyebrows are plasticine, as are his eyelids, which are separately molded in miniature press-molds and are only put on when he needs to blink. Whilst it is true that these shortcuts have enabled the studio to make some significant time savings, changing the beak or mouth on a model is a time-consuming process and one that needs to be carefully monitored and logged, since each character has between forty and sixty different mouth shapes with which to speak.

"M   I   ST   ER

MAC. RELAX | MAC. LONG Ai-E | MAC. WIDE Ai-E | MAC. BMP | MAC. FV | MAC. DST Z | MAC. KRNGY | MAC. OE(oh) SCOTLAND | MAC. L-TH | MAC. W-OO "STRONGER" O | MAC. TRUMPET OO MOOOO | MAC. UH

In addition to all the run-of-the-yard chickens, model-making is also responsible for building "specials," birds that for one reason or another are required to have a different look for a particular scene.

Take the sequence in which the chickens attempt to catapult Bunty into flight. In the script it says that "Bunty shoots forward. . . . She flaps furiously then— BLOOP!—slams into the fence. Her head pops through one of the links, she hangs there, nearly choking." As Bunty briefly flies her sizable bulk is first of all stretched and then squashed as it slams into the fence. This is an animation principle—aptly known as "squash and stretch"—that is reasonably easy to accomplish in line animation or, indeed,

with plasticine. But Bunty's body, being made of silicon, is a rigid shape with no ability to squash or stretch. The answer is to create what Jan Sanger calls "a special squashy Bunty" that will allow the distortions required in achieving the desired visual effect.

In addition to the main characters, *Chicken Run* features a number of crowd scenes requiring "background chickens" that can be categorized as falling into four types: "Chicken A" (the standard "extra"), "Chicken B" (with a shorter neck), "Chicken C" (taller than the others) and "Chicken D" (which is basically short and round). The most common extras are types A and B but in every dozen chickens you will usually find one C and a couple of Ds.

Rather than having to remodel a character's face for every word spoken, the animators have a series of replacement beaks (or mouths) representing the shapes formed in making particular sounds. The animator fits the beak to the face, blends in the plasticine, exposes a frame of film, removes and replaces the beak, and repeats the process. Above, beak shapes for Mac and a sketch by Nick titled "Willard Tweedy's Nervous Smiles." Below, Mrs. Tweedy's head pronounces the name of her better half.

121

T W EE DY!"

A quartet of "A's" in the model-making shop.

"We've got seventy-eight average background chickens," explains Jan, "and we don't have any spares. So we just need to keep on making chickens. We're turning out three or four of them a week. It's just like being on a constant conveyor belt."

This makes the model-making department sound not unlike a factory. Indeed, in the end it turns out that there are one hundred individual stages involved in the process of making an average chicken. Each armature can take three weeks to make, first in resin and then in metal, in order to be able to take the stress of animation. Casting molds of the body shapes, making the "skins" (roughly ten skins from each mold), and then removing the mold lines—a process called "seaming"—can take up to three or four days, after which the skins have to be fitted onto the armatures and painted. The head, wings, tail, legs, and leg fluffles, also have to be molded and painted.

Every Friday, production manager Harry Linden logs the following week's schedule on a series of huge boards showing how many animation units are working on which sequences and what puppets are required when and where. "We look at the board," says Jan, "and we say, 'Right, next week we need three Rockys for these scenes; and two Gingers and Buntys for those scenes.' We then give the modelers and press-molders the weekly shopping list. At any one time we're only a week in advance of the animators, so we quite often have to move people around, taking someone off less urgent work, for example, in order to help get extra puppets ready."

Although a lot of people are working at repetitive—some might think, routine—jobs, Jan is not keen on the factory analogy: "I think of it as being more like a workshop. Sometimes people who have been doing the same job for a long time get frustrated, but there's a lot of enthusiasm among people to be working on this film. And many of them are going places. It's possible to begin press-molding chicken beaks and move on to be an assistant animator. That's why I say it's not a factory: it's an environment in which people are creatively involved."

Creativity is certainly everywhere. And nowhere is it more evident than in the way the model makers solved the vexing problems of chicken puppets that matched Nick and Peter's conception of how they should look and move and were practical to build. It will be up to others to create the stage upon which these miniature actors must perform.

Those who work most closely with the averages have assigned them names: the A's, for example, include Alice, Agnes, Amber, and Annie. Story supervisor Bridget Mazzey says, "Walkie conversations can sound very bizarre: 'We need a Betty, a Doris, an A dark with a purple woolly, plus Babs with no knitting for unit 6 please.'"

Opposite: A singing group made up of three "B's" referred to in the studio as the Chicken Supremes! The hut is open at the top so that the scene can be lit and the animators can have easy access to the puppets. Note the disco ball in the top left corner. Each mirrored square has been altered to create round reflections in the room and a blob of putty that will be removed is visible on it.

Time for a backstage tour. . . . The vast storage space at Aardman's Aztec West studio is filled with lamps and lighting rigs and stacks of wooden staging on which the sets are erected, as well as many of the sets themselves, including the Tweedys' farmhouse. This is an outsized doll's house styled in Victorian Gothic with "a slightly *Psycho*-look" to create sinister, sharply angled outlines against the skyline.

"We work on two basic scales," explains Tim Farrington, who, with his partner, Phil Lewis, runs Farrington-Lewis, the firm that is building the sets and props for *Chicken Run.* "Tweedy world and chicken world. All the puppets are around twelve inches high, but the difference is that in the Tweedy world everything is built to look human scale, while in the chicken world everything has to be reduced to bird scale. Where it gets complicated is when the two worlds meet and you have a twelve-inch-high Mr. and Mrs. Tweedy and two-inch chickens."

Everything that is used or handled by any of the characters—human or chicken—has to fit with these scales, whether it's a newspaper for Mrs. Tweedy or a pair of suspenders stolen from Mr. Tweedy to be used as a method of propulsion for an escaping chicken. And with twelve-inch-high puppets, it is obviously impossible to use real objects. Hence the clutter that surrounds us: miniature barns, sheds and other farm buildings and a great many "bits of buildings" including doors, windows, pieces of roof, large sections of red brick walling, and lengths of drystone walls typical of the kind used on Yorkshire farms. Smaller objects are arranged in cardboard boxes stacked on several yards of metal shelving: tiny rakes, booms, buckets,

"Wing Commander T. I. Fowler, reporting for duty." **FOWLER**

In contrast to the warm wood-and-straw-filled world inhabited by the chickens, the Tweedys' world is comparatively dark and gloomy. With a barren tree in the background, the worn steps leading up to the front door, and the dimly lit, curtained windows, there are conscious echoes of those sinister hilltop houses featured in films such as Psycho and Salem's Lot. Here, set builders add finishing touches to the house at Aardman's Aztec West site.

Animating puppets on large sets often requires the animator to get into uncomfortable positions. Left, key animator Jason Spencer-Galsworthy is working on part of the sequence, illustrated opposite, when the circus man comes in search of the missing Rocky. The looming Tweedy house, with its lighted windows looking over the farmyard, is essential to the mood of the scene.

Echoes of Alfred Hitchcock: the dim Mr. Tweedy peers over the farmyard, puzzled by events he cannot quite understand.

 128

A moody inspirational sketch of the Tweedy farmhouse by Roger Hall. Like Mrs. Tweedy herself, it is gaunt, sharply angled, and very menacing.

Senior director of photography Dave Alex Riddett lighting a scene set in Mrs. Tweedy's office. Dave and the two other directors of photography working on Chicken Run *are responsible for creating the distinctive "look" of the finished picture. Note how close the camera, left, must be to the puppets.*

Mrs. Tweedy works on the account books surrounded by claustrophobic clutter including heavy furnishings, an ornate framed portrait, an ugly vase and a period telephone, adding machine and filing cabinet. Notice the Tweedy's wedding photograph on the bookshelf in the background. In an intentional violation of continuity, Peter Lord decided that it should migrate magically to the desk so that it can jump when Mrs. Tweedy slams her fist down.

10"

2½"

2"

2½"

The dining-room table is still laid with the remnants of the chicken dinner that was once called "Edwina." Below, a selection of props made from scratch for the set. On the dresser is a holiday snap of the Tweedys on the beach at the northern holiday resort of Blackpool. Note that Mr. Tweedy is the jackass!

16"

8"

8"

milk churns, and dustbins; small rusting water troughs and feed holders; scaled-down tractors, wheelbarrows, farm gates, and water pumps; miniature crates, barrels, and sacks of chicken feed.

Tim leads me past a huge model of the farmyard set, up-ended against a wall, creating a surreal effect with buildings, walls and fences jutting outward and various farm vehicles and an entire pond full of "water" bizarrely defying gravity. "Of course," says Tim, "Aardman is only able to achieve all this because the company managed to gear itself up to do so not just in terms of staff and infrastructure but also space." It is a view confirmed by David Sproxton when I run across him on his way to a production meeting. "It was a radical decision for us to move," he explains, "particularly since we originally thought we were going to build a new studio on a car park."

The parking lot in question was at Aardman's existing site at Gas Ferry Road, in another part of Bristol. "We were thinking that if we expanded the studio and reduced the number of commercials we were making there, we would have more than enough room in which to make the feature. How wrong we were!" The building, which was going to cost £2 million to build, was designed, and the diggers were about to start ripping up the lot when—after a further round of calculations—it was suddenly realized

that they really would not have sufficient space. In fact, they were out by as much as a factor of two or three. "Which was when," says David, "we decided to look for something else, found this site at Aztec West, and moved the feature and everyone working on it out here."

The decision to split up the production activities was not an easy one. The company had always been a family. From the days of the company's first studio in a former garage in Wetherall Place— where you had to duck your head as you entered—people got used to living cheek by jowl with one another, to sharing their ideas and inspiration as readily as they shared their plasticine.

With growing success came the decision to move to larger premises in Gas Ferry Road, but that same success meant more work and more staff and, again, less and less space. "Everyone was always crashing into each other," says David. "And it wasn't just that everyone was cramped, it was that everyone was constantly distracted, wanting to know what was going on, what everyone else was doing."

The move highlighted a significant difference between the way the company worked on relatively short-term projects like commercials as opposed to a feature film. "It is not uncommon," explains David, "for animators making a commercial to work until ten or eleven at night.

Phil Lewis (top) is looking at a camera set-up of the chicken coop scenes while Tim Farrington compares the blueprint for the pie machine with a preliminary scale model.

133

If it weren't for the bank of lights at the top of the photograph, opposite, the scene might pass for a typical idyllic landscape in the Yorkshire dales. It is, in fact, a set for the view beyond the fences of Tweedy's Farm which fires Ginger's desire for freedom. The set is constructed in sections with gaps to allow access for technicians—for example, between the first stone wall and the field beyond. The foreshortened perspective conceals such breaks and cheats the eye into thinking that the view is one that stretches for miles.

Standing beside a 20-by-10-foot canvas skyscape with clouds, Tim says, "I've just found out I've got to paint another four skies. I didn't know I had to do them till today! Still, one down, three to go." He has already painted 89 skies and will have done 120 of them by the time the film is completed.

134

10"

6"

14"

However, it is impossible to work at such intensity over a long period such as is involved in filming a feature. The folks doing the job are the same sort of people, it's the motivation that's different: making commercials is like being a sprinter, making a feature is like running a marathon: you really do have to pace yourself."

It has been a steep learning curve for everyone, not least Tim and Phil. They had both previously worked with Aardman and decided to join forces in order to service the studio's needs when they embarked on the making of a feature. "We knew that if Aardman made a feature," says Phil, who joins us and takes me on a tour of the rest of the sets while Tim gets on with painting a sky, "we could gear ourselves up to produce the sets and props. The only question was, were they really going to do it? Eventually, we decided that we really believed that *they* really believed that they really were going to make this film!"

For a year, Farrington-Lewis built test sets. "It was," says Phil, "essential that we should establish methods of working long before we started filming. We realized very early on that everything would

have to be made bigger and stronger and built to last longer." Despite all their preparation, Phil and Tim underestimated some aspects of the work. "At first," says Phil, "we had no idea how many times over we'd have to build the same set, simply because so many units were going to be working on almost identical scenes. We also rather underestimated the job of simply keeping track of everything: 'Will this set for Hut 17 be free in time to be used by another unit or are we going to have to make another one?'"

We reach the film's biggest set, running the full sixty-foot width of the studio: the entire chicken farm with all its huts and its perimeter fence and an astonishing, receding vista of fields, drystone walls, winding roads, gently sloping hills, distant moorlands with crags and rocky outcrops, and a utopian, blue-sky horizon that, for the restless Ginger, represents freedom.

It is a masterly illusion: standing outside the gates, you can look away into the distance seemingly for mile upon mile. Walk toward those green hills until they are almost within your reach, take another look, and you get a very different perspective on things. The countryside is

Creating a convincing atmosphere of place takes imagination and a great deal of planning. The process of giving three-dimensional reality to the sketches of Tweedy's Farm involved the making of a scale model (opposite). Shown below are finished models and a scale drawing for some of the many farmyard props. The photographs above give a glimpse of the detailing incorporated in the farmyard sets.

2"

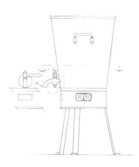

7"

constructed in parallel sections with access gaps running between this wall and that field, this fold in the valley and that steep incline. Walk back to where Mrs. Tweedy is parading up and down in front of the rows of terrified chickens and the scene recreates itself before your very eyes.

Tristan Oliver, one of the film's three directors of photography, is busily adjusting the lighting: "That sky is sixty feet wide," he explains, "which makes it very tricky to light. I'm using two very large lamps for the sun and the knack is to angle them so that you only get one shadow. I'm also bouncing a lot of light off the sky—rather like *real* sunlight does—in order to give a very naturalistic back-fill light."

The secret of the set is its sheer size. "We could have made the set much smaller and cheated perspective," says Tristan, "but the moment you move the camera the background appears to move too fast in comparison with the rest of the set and the illusion is shattered. This set is so large that you can virtually throw the camera around all over the place and perspectives look absolutely right." He sees this set as having a crucial importance for the film: "Since so many scenes are one-on-one close-up shots and even the wide shots tend to be crowded with thirty-plus chickens, it's vital to get a big vista into the film every now and again—it's like a much needed breath of air."

To point the contrast, Tristan takes me to see one of the many scenes that are being filmed inside Hut 17. "I love these

Careful not to disrupt the Lilliputian world of the farmyard set, trainee assistant animator Dave Bennett repositions Mrs. Tweedy in a scene in which she and her husband hold roll call for the chickens.

interiors: these wooden huts have such a cozy, intimate atmosphere and there are lots of light sources: candles and paraffin lamps making little pools of light that give the huts this warm, comfortable, timbery look." For Tristan one of the joys of his job is to be working on Farrington-Lewis's sets. "They are a joy to light," he says, "The textures are right; the whole feeling is right. You never have to make a

Unbeknownst to Mr. and Mrs. Tweedy, Hut 17 is the focal point of all the activities involved in the chickens' attempts to escape from the farm.

silk purse out of a sow's ear, never have to compromise yourself—you can only make the best of it."

Phil Lewis, who is also one of the film's art directors, takes me on to the design department, crowded with drawing boards and plan chests. Sliding open a drawer, Phil pulls out detailed plans of various buildings and farm equipment: "We've had to pay far greater attention to detailing because almost everything is made as if it might be seen in close-up." Everywhere are indications of how much detailed thought and work goes into creating even tiny moments in the film. Pinned to the wall is a simple layout of Hut 17, showing the sleeping arrangements—each nest marked with the name of its chicken occupant; on one drawing board are the samples of the rough "pin-bird" diagrams showing the escape plans devised by Ginger and the others; propped up on one of the plan chests are a couple of photographs: one shows Mr. and Mrs. Tweedy on their wedding day (cutting a cake that is topped off with a chicken decoration), the other is a holiday snap taken on the Tweedys' honeymoon at the northern seaside resort of Blackpool.

Opposite: The interior sets for Hut 17 feature in a number of the film's key scenes, including the one where Ginger alerts her companions to the fact that the Tweedys have invested in a machine for making chicken pies. Not too surprisingly, perhaps, one of the background birds has already lost her head! Actually, the explanation for the headless chicken is simple: since, on screen, this bird will only be seen from the neck down, there was no need to give her her head and there was one less startled expression needing to be animated. Meanwhile, the remaining chickens' horrified expressions are heightened by the lighting rig, bottom.

An early sketch by Michael Salter of a "modern chicken coop" that is beginning to look like the Hut 17 of the finished film. Notice the various chicken activities going on: sleeping, thinking, reading, smoking, yo-yoing, playing card games, and attempting to keep the place spick and span!

GINGER: "Time is of the essence. We have to get out before that wretched machine is up and running."

Sack for covering
Fowler

HUT 17

Back wall of hut – Swirelling

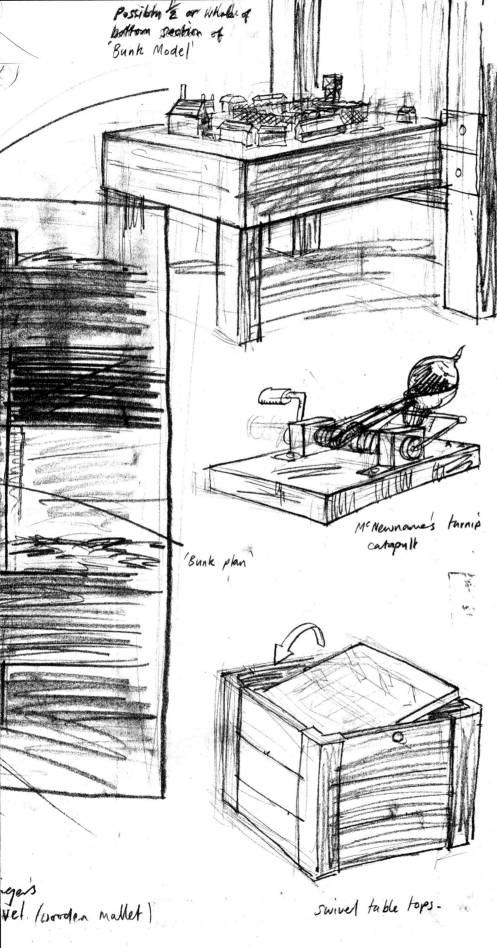

Possibly ½ or whole of bottom section of 'Bunk Model'

'Bunk plan'

Mc Newname's turnip catapult

...ger's

...vel. (wooden mallet)

swivel table tops.

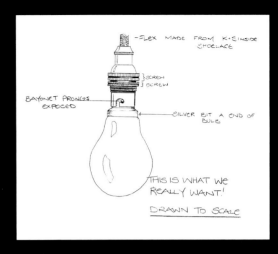

FLEX MADE FROM K·S INSIDE SHOELACE

SCREW
SCREW

BAYONET PRONGS EXPOSED

SILVER BIT A END OF BULB

THIS IS WHAT WE REALLY WANT!

DRAWN TO SCALE

This atmospheric sketch of the interior of Hut 17 by Michael Salter and Roger Hall shows some of the cunning methods employed by the chickens to secrete details of the various escape plans in case one of the Tweedys should come poking about. Every detail of every set— however small—has to be carefully worked out, drawn and made: even a simple electric light-bulb (above, drawn by Matt Perry) has to be constructed from scratch in order to appear to be in scale with the rest of the set.

Above, Hut 17 goes through various stages of construction at the workshop of Farrington-Lewis. Huts that are seen only in long shots are entirely made from a single mold, but those in foreground and close-up shots are constructed from a series of molded units comprising walls and floors, with doors and windows that open and close on tiny, handmade hinges. A completed set (far right) for the interior of one half of Hut 17 allows the animators access to the central section of the hut. The nests were all pre-made as boxes fitted with "cast straw interiors" and embellished with advertisements for "Pete's Farmhouse Produce," as an indication that the penny-pinching Tweedys have built their chicken nests from old fruit and vegetable crates.

142

Opposite: Nick and Fetcher supply a radio to provide music for the dance held in Hut 17. Notice the false ceiling cut with irregular holes used to create lighting effects inside the hut and the chicken to the right supported by rigging rather than legs. A chicken's body is just visible to the far right: it is positioned in front of the set, which is capped with a piece of unfinished wood. This bird will appear to be in the scene from the point of view of the movie camera.

Animator Seamus Malone works on a complex scene in Hut 17, involving a large number of chicken actors.

ROCKY: That's called a beat, sister. Feel it pulsing through your body?

BUNTY: Yes. Pulsing. Fancy that.

ROCKY: Hey, well then go with it, baby.

BUNTY: Oh my. Look. I'm "going with it!"

BABS: Bunty! What's got into you!

BUNTY: Same thing that's got into you apparently!

ROCKY: Just go with the flow, gals! Let it go!

145

Watched by Mac, Bunty and the others, Rocky and Babs take to the dance floor! Note that the chicken to the right is being supported by rigging, which will not be visible in the scene. An ordinary carpenters' c-clamp, right, establishes a sense of the scale of the scene. The roof of the hut remains open to allow for lighting and access by the animators.

ROCKY: Atta girl, Babsy!

MR. TWEEDY: Er . . . what is it?

MRS. TWEEDY: It's a pie machine, you idiot. Chickens go in, pies come out.

MR. TWEEDY: What kind of pies?

MRS. TWEEDY: Apple.

MR. TWEEDY: My favorite!

146

MRS. TWEEDY: Chicken pies, you great lubbox!

MR. TWEEDY: How does it work?

MRS. TWEEDY: Get me a chicken and I'll show you.

MR. TWEEDY: I know just the one.

The pie machine is not simply the means of achieving one of the great animation set pieces in Chicken Run, *it is also something of a symbol: representing both the promise (and the threat) of mechanization. From the first moment Mrs. Tweedy sees the machine in a catalogue, she is impressed by the sleekness of its modernity: it is clearly a techno-logical miracle. However, for Rocky and Ginger, trapped inside the pie machine, opposite, the miracle is that they not only survive, but that they wreak havoc with the innards of the mechanical marvel. A sequence like this is very tricky to animate: rigging needed to suspend objects in space is visible at the top of the photograph.*

Tim Farrington arrives from painting skies to take me to Farrington-Lewis's South Bristol premises, a twenty-minute car ride from Aztec West, where the interior of the pie machine is being put together. "We are illusionists!" says Tim, as he shows me into the workshops where more than fifty people are hard at work. "The illusion is one of blending the cartoony with the realistic. That is the great appeal of Nick and Peter's films: they are a mix of tangible reality with a comic, romantic element. People relate to that style and we have to create that look in three dimensions."

To do this, the set builders at Farrington-Lewis make use of anything and every-thing. They collect and keep any number of found objects ("scrapyards," says Tim, "are a goldmine") some of these bits and pieces get used as they are, others have to be adapted: "You develop an eye for looking at something and imagining how it could be turned into something else."

More often than not, however, things are built from scratch using the lathes, drills, saws, sanders, milling machines, and vacuum-form machines that fill the site with a cacophony of high-decibel sounds. "You can often waste a lot of time," says Tim, "trying to adapt something that is

almost there—only to find that it's made out of some uncomfortable material which it is difficult to paint or glue things to." One solution to this problem is to make a mold of the object and then cast it in more modeler-friendly material. Tim hands me a cogwheel that is going to be part of the pie machine: it has been cast in polyurethane and made in a mold. But the mold, on this occasion, was not made from a *real* cog but one specially carved from wood to the dimensions needed for the machine. "We silver spray-paint it to make it look as if its made of metal and then scrub it down to take the shine off it. Finally we rub it over with lead grate polish which gives it the look of age and use. It's details like this that give the film a credible appear-ance. It takes a little longer to make things from scratch when it might have been possible to find something that already existed and which was almost right. The trouble is, we have learnt from bitter experience that things that are *almost* right are never *really* right."

That said, nothing here is ever thrown away: "You chuck something out that may have been lying around for ages and what happens? Two days later you wish you still had it. So we keep anything that,

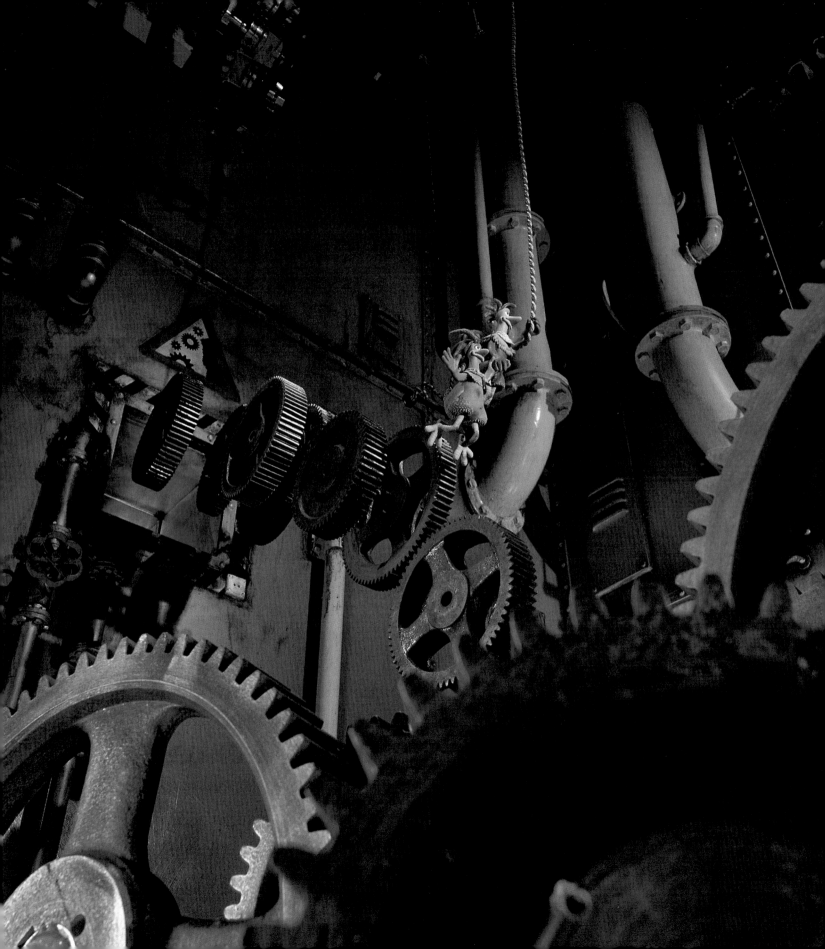

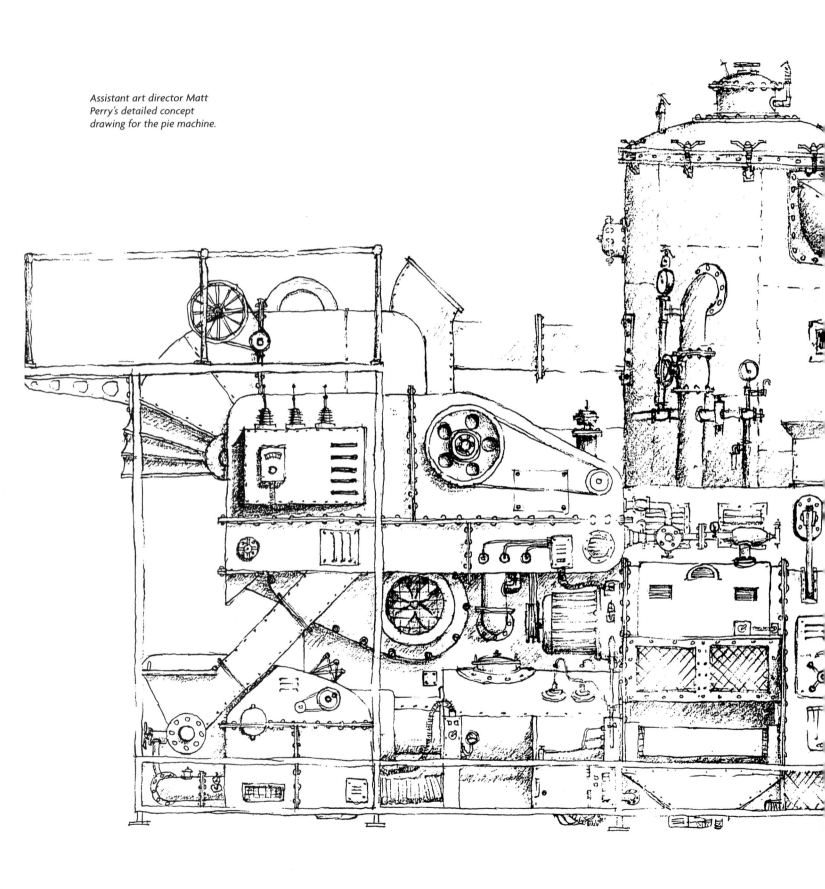

Assistant art director Matt Perry's detailed concept drawing for the pie machine.

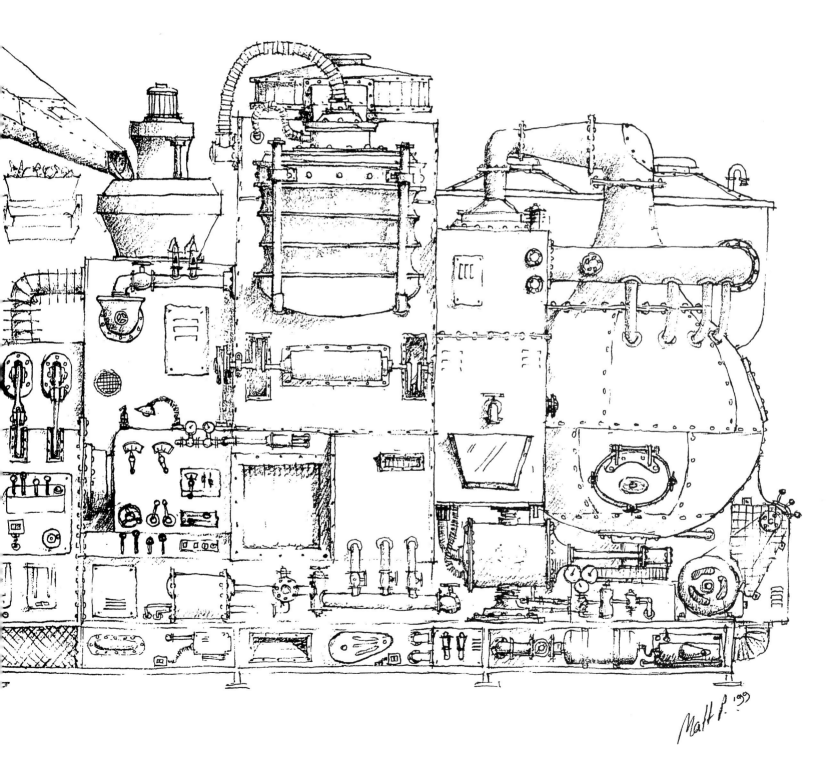

Matt P. '99

The pie machine is first mocked up in cardboard at the workshops of Farrington-Lewis. This model can be photographed from all angles, with puppets standing in for scale, to give an early indication of how specific moments in the sequence will look.

150

however unlikely, may one day come in useful." As with just about everything in an Aardman film, deception is the name of the game: I pick up a length of chain and am surprised to discover that it is rigid—a long stick of chain links. "It has to be like that," explains Tim, "because when it's in the machine, the chain has to look as if it is under tension and if the links were loose they might move between shots." I assume that the chain has also been cast from scratch, but I am wrong. "Not this time!" laughs Tim. "That's a *real* chain, we just welded the links together."

There is an ad-hoc improvisational approach to problem solving here that recalls the do-it-yourself inventiveness demonstrated by Wallace and Gromit in Nick Park's earlier films. Indeed, warehouse manager Jak Goodyear, who is working on a milling machine turning a standard piece of rigging into a gadget for lifting the pans inside the pie machine, empathizes with the creator of the Techno-Trousers and the Knit-O-Matic machine: "Oh, yes!" he says, "We relate to Wallace all right—we're always making things fit, bodging things, and lashing them together." "Fortunately," adds Tim, "the beauty of film is that

some of these gadgets really do only have to last long enough to be captured on film."

Scenic painter Francesca Maxwell is experimenting with sample surfaces for the interior of the oven: creating, by hand, a black-and-white polka-dotted look that suggests enameling. Having tried various intensities of speckling, she is about to start work on the actual surfaces of the oven set. "I put some spots on, let it dry, add more, till either it has the desired look or I'm seeing spots before the eyes." Model maker Gavin Richards is adapting a gauge to be used on the pie machine that will need an indicator that can be gradually moved by the animator during filming as the pressure in the gravy vat builds toward the bursting point.

The interior of the pie machine is being assembled in the next room: it is an impressive bulk of pale-green enameled and stainless-steel machinery. "Of course," says Tim, "its not made of metal at all but our own secret formula which is—wood! We use plywood and a lot of the utterly magical MDF (medium density fibreboard), which is just compressed wood sheeting but which, unlike ordinary

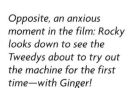

Opposite, an anxious moment in the film: Rocky looks down to see the Tweedys about to try out the machine for the first time—with Ginger!

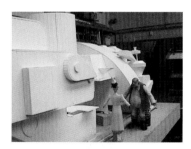

ROCKY: Whoa. Look at the size of that thing.

The pie machine was deliberately designed as a vast, complicated-looking contraption, covered with levers, switches, and gears, buttons, knobs, pipes, and pistons.

wood, keeps its shape, has no telltale grain marks and takes all kinds of paint and, best of all, can end up looking as if it was metal."

The interior has the conveyor belt on which Ginger and Rocky find themselves sprinting—Indiana Jones–style—in order to escape a giant roller. The belt contains metal sheeting for puppets magnetized feet, and all the gears and other parts have been cast either from real pieces of equipment or ones that have been specially carved. The nuts, bolts, and rivets have also been cast and are popped into drilled holes as a finishing touch. "They don't do anything," laughs Tim, "they just look good."

As Tim Farrington demonstrates how the machine comes apart into sections to give access to the animators for filming shots from different angles, Model-maker Lisa Scantlebury brings in the finishing touch: an oval manufacturer's plaque to be "bolted" onto the exterior of the machine. Made in MDF with individually hand-carved letters glued on and then painted to look as if it were made in steel, the words read: "Poultry Products, Est. 1901."

Scattered about in odd corners of the factory are rejected scale models of the chicken-powered flying machine, called the crate, in which the chickens will make their grand escape. They are reminders that this is Farrington-Lewis's next big project to tackle.

As Tim is seeing me out, we pass his office. "Everything, but *everything* we have done on *Chicken Run* has been carefully recorded," he says. "We have logged every spring and sprocket we have made. Everything can be reproduced, anytime—however many years down the line. So, if Aardman ever decides to make *Chicken Run II*, Farrington-Lewis are ready!"

Before *that* day comes, however, the animators have to finish making the first *Chicken Run*.

Tim holds the plaque in place to assess the effect: "It's little touches like this," he says "that really lift the whole thing. Who notices these details, you might ask, but we believe people would notice if they weren't there."

As Rocky and Ginger are thrown free of the machine, Mr. Tweedy stares in dismay at a row of bristling levers whose functions clearly elude him—as well they might, since they have none! Right, supervising animator Loyd Price working on the scene.

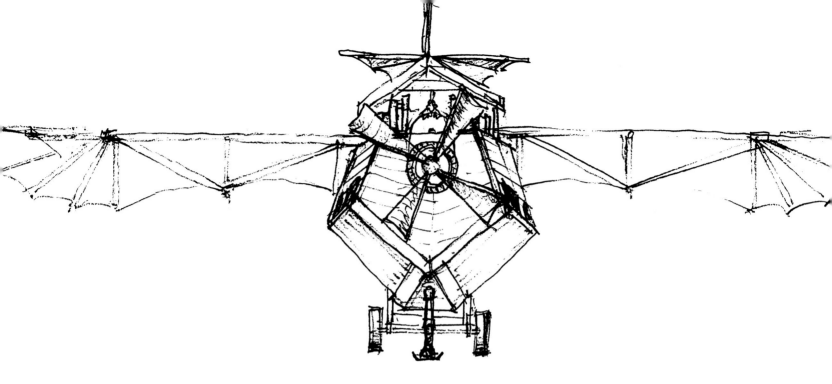

"What we were hoping to achieve," says Phil Lewis, "is something that will look extraordinary and funny: an old crate of a plane filled with chickens peddling like crazy. There are going to be at least sixty chickens inside that set. It has to look as if every chicken on the farm has got away."

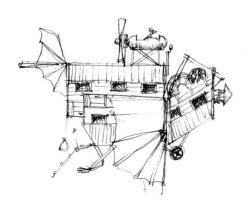

Early sketches for the crate, by Nick Park.

Nick P.   23 July '97

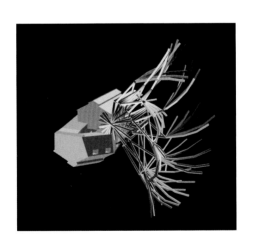

The crate is the last major set to be designed for the film. Computer simulations of the crate (above) and its wing movements (far left), from a concept design by Matt Perry, help the set-builders plan the model. Left, set production co-ordinator John Pealing builds a model of the crate at Farrington-Lewis.

It is night. Rocky is sitting on the rooftop of one of the corner huts in Tweedy's farm. In his hand he holds the badge presented to him by Fowler in recognition of his undoubted bravery in rescuing Ginger from the pie machine. Suddenly, Ginger is there beside him, and they begin a conversation that shows us how these two characters now view one another and how the events they have just been through have affected their relationship. Both of them have something to say: Ginger wants to apologize to Rocky and to thank him. Rocky, on the other hand, has decided it is time to own up and tell Ginger the truth—that he cannot fly.

Although the entire sequence on the rooftop comprises just over two pages of script, the animation—when finished—will have taken key animator Guionne Leroy five months to complete: "It's hard to sustain your vision for a sequence over such a long period; it tends to be more organic. There are times when you are inspired and others when you are so tired that you just keep going by sheer willpower."

It's a difficult scene, two chickens sitting and talking. Just sitting a chicken on a roof, it turns out, isn't that easy. If the birds were *real*, their weight would make them sink *into* the roof—an illusion that might easily be achieved if the puppets' bodies were made of plasticine that could be squashed into the right position. But these bodies are made out of silicon, which means that they have no "give" in them. The result looks wrong. Rocky and Ginger seem to be *balanced*—rather than really *sitting*—on the roof. The solution proves simple: carve semicircular chunks out of the roof ridge and then sit the chickens in the resulting hollows. Suddenly, they look as if they really *are* sitting on the roof.

"Chickens go in, pies come out." MRS. TWEEDY

The fact that the chickens do a lot of talking also presents its challenges: not only does Guionne have to synchronize their beak movements to a great many words; she also has to convey Rocky and Ginger's awkward, slightly embarrassed, shyly romantic mood.

Furthermore, there is an eloquence about Ginger's silence: "What I like about Ginger," says Guionne, "is that she is so feisty and driven that she seems selfish, hard, and lacking in compassion, although she is not. She doesn't realize that her drive comes across that way. It's the flaw in her personality that makes her "human." Thanks to Rocky, she becomes aware of it. In the scene on the roof, however, she is really cute and completely *unaware* that she is *being* cute—and that's attractive."

These are subtle emotions to convey with a piece of plasticine, and especially given the chickens' inherent design: their big eyes and beaks. The challenge facing all the animators on *Chicken Run* is to take their own feelings for the dialogue and then translate them from a human body and face into those of a chicken. "It's easier to shoot action than it is to shoot acting," says supervising animator Loyd Price. "Action is easier to get right. It's a lot less ambiguous. You can say: 'Bunty is catapulted through the air, she is flying along and her arms are flapping,' and there's a lot less room for error. When you're talking about acting and emotion—like the sequence with Rocky and Ginger on the roof—that's full of ambiguity. If that sequence had not been so well animated, it would have just fallen totally flat and then there'd be a big hole in the movie."

In other words, the puppets, and by extension, the animators, must be skilled actors. Although animators at Aardman have always acted out scenes to one another in preparation for doing the actual animation, they now also video-tape their rehearsals, along with the demonstrations given by the directors. "We used to act a scene," says Loyd, "and then you'd animate it and Nick would look at what you'd done and say, 'I didn't quite mean that. . . .' But now, we have it on video, so we can say, 'But that's exactly what you *did*, Nick!' So, the video rehearsal takes the ambiguity out of it."

"The fact that you can try three or four different ways of acting a shot very quickly before deciding which to animate is its greatest advantage," Loyd continues. "After you've done the rehearsal, you sit down with the director and discuss what works and what doesn't. The animator must really be in tune with what the director is expecting to see, so that by the time you are going for a take, you should really know the shape of the shot, the rhythm, the pace. There's generally

159

```
                    ROCKY
    Yeah, well um...it's just that, you
    know -- life -- as I've experienced it,
    you know -- out there, lone free
    ranging and stuff-- it's full of
    disappointments.

                    GINGER
    You mean, grass isn't all it's cracked
    up to be?

                    ROCKY
    Grass. Exactly. It's always greener
    on the other side. And then you get
    there and, and, and it's brown and
    prickly, you know what I mean?

    She shakes her head no.

                    ROCKY (cont'd)
    It's...it's like when I was a little
    chicklet. Just a little squirt, afraid
    of my own shadow, and my dad tells me
    he'll protect me because he's got magic
    powers. But as it turned out, he was
    just a regular rooster, you see what
    I'm saying?

    She nods - then shakes her head no.  Rocky sighs.

                    ROCKY (cont'd)
    What I'm trying to say is...
            (he looks deep into her eyes)
    Um...that is...
            (he caves)
    You're welcome.

    She smiles - and kisses his cheek.  There's a pause like that
    kiss might turn into more, then they both become uncomfortable.
    She turns back toward the hill.
```

Rocky and Ginger have a moonlit talk on the roof of one of the huts: a short scene that took five months to put onto film. One look at the stage directions for a portion of the scene in the script (above) explains why. In one brief passage, the characters are given a series of subtle gestures to perform.

Although animation at Aardman remains a hand-made operation, the studio uses computer technology both to help with the planning of sequences and to enhance the visual look of sequences. In this scene an attempt is being made to catapult Bunty into flight, using a nest on wheels (right). After a computer simulation is prepared by Darren Dubicki (above), the scene is animated with models (below left) using photographic technology

(below center) to blur the image and suggest speed. Once Bunty is in flight, the puppet must be supported with rigging (below right). The rigging is digitally removed in postproduction, so that she appears to be flying absolutely unaided (opposite). When, a few seconds later, Bunty crashes into the wire fencing, a special puppet is substituted for the standard Bunty in order to create the comic effect of a chicken being, momentarily, squashed!

Key animators Suzy Fagan (right) and Jason Spencer-Galsworthy (below) animating scenes featuring Rocky and Ginger.

"All you can do is work with the puppet and see what happens," says Guionne Leroy. "You may start out doing one thing and change your mind because the puppet seems to be going in a different direction. Every animator will tell you that there are times when it feels as if it has a will of its own."

something in a shot that is a key element, the reason why that shot is *in* the movie. It is all about hitting on that one thing. It will be about making the acting point in the scene, making that connection with the audience, getting the thought across. Hit that, and the rest will follow."

For Guionne Leroy, the knack of being able to act in animation is instinctive: "It works best when I don't try to think. When I've acted out enough I know the feeling I'm trying to create, but when I begin animating I usually try to start afresh—from the chicken itself. And I really try to let the puppet *act*, to direct me how and where to move it. All you can do is work with the puppet and see what happens. You may start out doing one thing and change your mind because the puppet seems to be going in a different direction. Every animator will tell you that there are times when it feels as if it has a will of its own."

The set for Leroy's rooftop scene is in one small corner of the area occupied by the studios at Aztec West. A vast space has been partitioned off into a series of booths or units: nothing luxurious, just small, plain wooden boxes of varying sizes. It's not very big, consisting of just the roof to the hut, behind which is one of Tim Farrington's painted backgrounds of a night sky with gauzy cloud effects and tiny electric stars. There are also a number of lamps lighting the scene, the camera, and, of course, two chickens. A black curtain is draped across the doorway, making the "room" hot and claustrophobic.

Lighting this scene has not been easy. "Actually," says Tristan Oliver, "it's a bit of a pain. If it really were nighttime in the Yorkshire Dales in the 1950s, then it would be completely *black*. There is no

163

Loyd Price positions Ginger in the menacing shadow cast by a cutout of Mrs. Tweedy.

light up there at night. So you are creating a lighting situation that doesn't truly exist. And you are working with directors and animators who are keen on showing the characters' faces. In live action you can get away without seeing faces—a glint on an eyeball is enough to tell you that someone is there in the darkness. In animation that is much harder, you need to see faces—and *teeth*, except that these chickens have big sticking-out beaks that cast enormous shadows so that you can't easily *see* their teeth. Basically, therefore, you are trying to light the scene as if it wasn't lit—or, as if it was illuminated by this extraordinary large, always *blue*, moon." Despite those drawbacks, the desired lighting was eventually achieved and Guionne is working away on the slow, step-by-step process of making two puppets relate to one another in a way audiences will accept—and believe.

For many years drawn animation has made use of a process called "rotoscoping" in which sequences in an animated film are filmed first in live action and the footage studied—and sometimes directly traced—in order to create the line images that appear on screen. It is not possible to use live-action film this way when making a model-animated film, but a great deal of reference footage is shot in order to guide or inspire the animators. Here, senior set dresser Manon Roberts and assistant art director Matt Perry are being filmed dancing together by Loyd Price, who is crouching in the foreground watching a monitor. The video will be an aid for animating the dance scene in Hut 17, opposite.

The area between these little studios is a beamed and battened wooden maze with an authentic "behind-the-set" look found in a live-action film studio: on one side the magic; on the other, the commonplace. Wandering this labyrinth and peeping behind the black curtains is an extraordinary experience. On one set, Mrs. Tweedy is standing within the imposing shadow of the pie machine, her hands itching to get at the controls; on another, Ginger is addressing the escape committee in Hut 17; and on still another Ginger and Rocky are peering round the corner of a hut as the circus van pulls up. So many different scenes from different parts of the film, all being brought simultaneously to life by different hands. It is a stunning feat of organization.

Leaving the sets, climbing the circular staircase and passing through the canteen where the catering staff are getting ready for another lunchtime invasion, you come to the office of production manager, Harry Linden. This is the eye of the storm, the Aardman equivalent of Mission Control. Between crackly conversations on his walkie-talkie—speaking to forty-five people throughout the studio—Harry takes me through the complex system that ensures that the film remains on course, on time, and, hopefully, on budget. It is all regulated on the schedule board. In fact, there are *six* boards, twelve sides, divided into a complex grid that is pinned with hundreds of color-coded pieces of paper from which—at a glance—Harry can tell who is working where and on what.

Twenty-two units are currently engaged on the film, divided into teams responsible to one of the two directors. A mass of little triangles pinned to the board represent the animators: red for Peter Lord's team, yellow for Nick Park's. The scenes being filmed by these units are indicated with extracts from the storyboard, along with details of set, props, and puppet requirements. If something goes wrong—a puppet gets broken, a scene begins to overrun or turns out to be more involved than had been expected—then Harry can bring a different scene into production or switch an animator from one scene to another.

What is astonishing is that Aardman has the personnel to operate so many animation units. Before *Chicken Run*, the studio boasted some of the finest animation talent in the business, but it did not have enough skilled animators to maintain Aardman's other work *and* launch into the making of a feature-length film. In 1996, anticipating the increased numbers of animators needed to make *Chicken*

On one of the soundstages, Suzy Fagan watches a video playback of a scene between Rocky and Ginger which she has been animating. It is an opportunity for an animator to see how a scene plays.

The film progresses by slow, micro-measurable degrees: the most seconds shot in a day have been, to date, twenty-six, that is, less than half a minute of the completed film. In a good week, the studio succeeds in turning out two minutes. At this rate, daily, weekly, and monthly schedules must be meticulously maintained. If the overall filming schedule slips so much as a half day in a week, that half day has, somehow, got to be pulled up again.

Gradually, the final film takes shape, as scene by scene the story reel—which contains the whole movie from beginning to end—becomes more polished. This is done in editorial, using a computer system called Avid, which carries the storyboard, dialogue, music, and effects, as well as finished footage.

For example, when an animator is rehearsing a scene, the animation is recorded on video from a video camera (a "video assist") attached to the film camera. This video recording can be edited into the story reel so that the animation can be studied in context and, if necessary, changed or corrected before the final filming on 35mm film.

Run, Aardman ran two six-month training courses in association with the University of Western England. Of the ten people who attended the course, nine are now working for the studio.

Loyd Price, who led the training, is proud of the fact that those animators are now contributing to *Chicken Run*: "When we were training people we didn't actually know how many people we would have animating. The trainees might just have been assistants helping what we initially thought would be a team of about six animators. But it soon became clear we needed all the help we could get, and those original trainees are now animating. They were thrown straight into the deep end and are making a vital contribution to the film."

Alternatively, it might be a complicated scene that is being planned with the help of a computer. By pre-visualizing a scene using computer graphics, it is possible to calculate the dimensions of the set and the best angles from which the sequence can be filmed. As a result, only that part of the set which will be seen on screen needs to be built. There was a time when a cardboard mock-up of a particular set would have been built and laid out on the studio floor—or, if the set was too big, in the studio parking lot—and cut-out, stand-up figures would be moved about

to see how the scene might look. "We'd all be crowding round this mock-up," recalls art director Phil Lewis, "wandering about with tape measures and viewfinders trying to calculate how far a character would walk in a given number of seconds. Now we can do it in the computer which is quicker and easier."

"You can know what a scene looks like as a series of drawings," says Peter Lord, "but since drawings can cheat *frighteningly*, that's where the machine can help." For Nick, the computer is an invaluable aid: "I have to say, I still prefer to look at a storyboard when it comes to character because you don't get the same sense of personality from an image on a computer screen, but for action scenes it is indispensable, not just for working out how big a set you have to build and how much studio space it will take up, but also for changing angles and tweaking cuts."

Until they are replaced by animation footage, these computer tests—precise, yet so much more "plastic-looking" than the real animation—will be stored onto the story reel via the editing machine, allowing the sequence to be viewed within the context of the whole film. In many instances there will be also be more than one take of a shot and these will all be located at the correct point within the story line so that they can be compared alongside each other at the tap of a key. The aim is, shot by shot, to replace the story sketches, video, and computer images with final footage. One of Harry Linden's small-yet-satisfying pleasures is the moment when a finished scene is passed by the directors and can be stamped "approved." When that happens, the completed scene will be cut into the story reel.

Trainee assistant animator Francesca Ferrario preps a puppet of Mrs. Tweedy for photography.

The animation units of the two directors each comprise seven key animators working with various combinations of three to four animators, two to four assistant animators, and five trainee animators. There is also a mass of people referred to as "cross-team players" who have to serve all the units, with jobs ranging from the three directors of photography, art directors, gaffers, riggers, chippies, and a puppet-wrangler.

Of these, the work of the directors of photography is key to how the film looks up on the screen. "Every film needs balance, variety, texture to keep the audience interested." says Dave Alex Riddett, senior director of photography. "Every sequence in a film—it might be happy, sad, or mysterious—helps tell the overall story, and the photographic look of those sequences is vitally important."

It might be the contrast of moonlight and shadow in the farmyard at night; the flickering candle lights in Hut 17 by which the escape committee make their covert plans; the clinical glare of the interior of the pie machine, or the depressing gloom within the Tweedy farmhouse. Every place, every scene, has a "look" and that

Computer simulations—such as these CGI pictures by Darren Dubicki of Ginger and the other chickens in the farmyard—are used to help in designing sets and planning animation.

On these two pages, a storyboard sequence from the pie machine escape showing Rocky plugging a potentially lethal gravy squirter with a carrot is contrasted with the same frames rendered in computer graphics. The storyboard drawings, by David Bowers, capture the drama of the moment. The computer images, opposite, by Darren Dubicki, lack the qualities that make the storyboard expressive, but they clearly delineate proportions and volumes that will help the set designers and animators in their work.

*Rocky plugs the gravy
squirter: the perspective in
this image from the final
film is remarkably similar
to the computer-generated
image of the same frame
on the previous page.*

going on, but also in determining their emotional response to what they see. "Strong black shadows," explains Dave Alex, "unusual camera angles, camera moves that gradually reveal the scene, all these create a feeling of tension or mystery such as in the opening sequence to *Chicken Run.*"

Just as in a Hitchcock thriller, shadows create powerful feelings of fear or uncertainty, so different lighting effects evoke other responses. "Softer lighting, warm colors, subtle shadows," says Dave Alex, "give a more cozy, intimate feel to the hut interiors. While bright colors picked out in a strong key light and shadows lifted with a full light tend to emphasize feelings of optimism and excitement in such scenes as those in which the chickens are engaged in flight training."

Lighting in model animation, Frank points out, follows the same basic principles as in live-action moviemaking: "Times of day and, of course, the type of weather can be used to great advantage in accentuating the drama. Although we probably indulge ourselves in these conventions to some extent, we always try to maintain an overall degree of realism which is applied to the project as a whole. The prime aim in this film is that all of our characters (despite being made of silicon and plasticine) should be presented as living beings with whom we can become emotionally involved. Therefore, a degree of naturalism is important, and if we were to shoot in an over-stylized way, for example, we could easily jeopardize that."

look is created by Dave Alex and the other directors of photography (or "DoP's"), Tristan Oliver and Frank Passingham.

The lighting for a scene and the way in which the camera is used to put that scene onto film are vital not simply in helping the audience understand what is

"The directors are more concerned with performance and cutting and they really only direct the lighting when it obviously conflicts with continuity," reflects

Tristan. "Consequently we tend to create a look which pleases us." Those results will enhance a scene, but, as Dave Alex explains, lighting effects must never get in the way of putting that scene onto film: "Lights and 'flags' (used to hold back the light) have to be carefully placed on a set in order to allow the animator full access to the characters. It's no use having the most beautifully lit set if the animator cannot perform his or her art with ease. Small sets can be particularly difficult to light; sometimes, where we are trying get light into a really confined space, we even have to use mirrors and 'reflect' the light into the set."

The scale of animation presents other difficulties. "The size of characters," says Tristan, "often means that they have to be placed very close to the camera lens in order to appear the correct size against a background. At these distances the range of focus or depth of field is very limited and can only be overcome by drastically decreasing the lens aperture. Although this ensures a focussed picture with a sense of depth, it requires either a lot of light or a very long shutter speed. Fortunately, because our cameras do not run continuously, we have a lot of control over what shutter speeds we use and these can be as long as four seconds."

Longer shutter speeds means lower light levels, which is fortunate for both the "actors" and the animators, as Tristan points out: "a lot of hot light can lead to melting models—and animators!"

Meltdown isn't the only issue involved in working with characters made out of plasticine, as Tristan explains: "Since it doesn't react like human skin and since the puppets are not humanoid, great care

has to be taken in order to light them sympathetically."

Continuity is of paramount importance: "Most shots," Dave Alex explains, "are filmed out of sequence, with sometimes months separating the filming of shots from the same scene. Many sets are duplicated to increase the work output, as well as being repeated in different scales. Great care must be taken, therefore, to match the lighting. Careful note taking, lighting diagrams, and a 'sensitive eye' when analyzing rushes, are all necessary to maintain a visual flow."

Such preparations are essential because, as Tristan points out, "There are no 'second takes' in animation. Everything has to be got right the first time and everything must be completely ready when the animator steps up to shoot. For this reason the degree of care is far greater than in live action where any errors can be dealt with a simple 'take two.'"

Although the DoP's have almost as much impact on the overall look of the completed film as the picture's directors, it is nevertheless crucial that the lighting cameramen be aware of exactly how Nick and Peter want to approach every scene.

"When you are working with Nick and Pete," says Frank, "there is no difficulty in understanding what they have in their mind's eyes. They know the project inside out and back to front and have no problem about giving you whatever information you need in order to be able to set up a shot. It is essential to get as much information from the directors as possible and it's not always wise simply to follow the storyboards, as there may have been recent changes to the

ever coming up to them and asking them about this or that. By keeping interruptions away it allows them the time they need to do their thinking."

Harry's control in relation to production issues is absolute. Peter and Nick's days are divided, one-third/two-thirds, between editorial work and directing. The day begins with a review of the previous day's "rushes," the shots which have been filmed, developed, and are being looked at to see whether they can be approved or whether they are going to have to be re-shot. Nick says, "We're always under pressure to approve stuff and you really do need to have very good reasons not to do so." The directors will also view the videotaped tests and then discuss the rehearsals with the animators, looking for ways in which a shot might be refined or improved before final animation begins.

The other two-thirds of the day are spent with the animation units on the studio floor. And that time is itself divided into half-hour segments that cannot overrun. Steering the two directors round the studio and through their daily schedule are a first, second, or third assistant director. Nick and Peter have found it hard to adapt to the system. "You really have to keep your wits about you," says Peter. "You're talking to an animator about one scene and then someone suddenly says, 'Quick! Off to Unit 23!' and you think to yourself, 'What the hell's Unit 23?' And it's not until you go through the curtain to Unit 23 that you

Peter Lord (left) discussing a scene with key animator Merlin Crossingham in which Fowler tries to assert his authority by getting the chickens lined up for roll call.

172

sequence or the director may have a last-minute idea for a way to enhance the scene."

In the end, of course, everyone turns to the directors, and a blur of activity surrounds Peter and Nick. *Chicken Run* is their film, it is based on their shared vision and it is natural that members of staff should want to seek their advice or opinion on anything and everything affecting the film. With so much going on this is not so easy. "We have to establish a positive, healthy environment in which the directors can be creative," Harry Linden says. "When Peter and Nick walk this building alone, people are for-

"Sometimes," says Nick, "you look at a shot and you have these niggling doubts about it: 'Can it be done better, or can't it? Can we afford the delay and the expense of animating it all over again?'"

remember what's going on there, by which time you are being expected to talk intelligently about it."

"I'm always reluctant to get pushed into doing the next job," adds Nick, "because I really haven't had time to think a minute ahead, and yet, within five minutes, I find I'm completely involved." The same thing happens all over again, and there's this constant switching of concentration and focus."

"It's terribly demanding," continues Peter, "because you have got to know where you are in the film, and not just geographically but also emotionally. You try to recall anything important you were thinking about a particular scene and then communicate that to somebody else with as much energy and force as you can muster—because it all depends on that."

The tentlike area where the animators prepare their puppets and the assistant directors hold court is called Town Square. Here are Nick Basche, trainee second assistant; Will Norie, third assistant director; and Merriel Waggoner, second unit second assistant director.

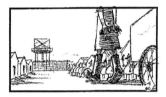

One day I spend an hour trying to keep up with Peter on his rounds. Nick hurries past the set of the farm and surrounding countryside, like Gulliver walking through Lilliput, while we stop off to talk with key animator Merlin Crossingham who is working on the "roll call" scene, in which Mrs. Tweedy strides into the compound to inspect the 150 chickens who are lined up in front of their huts. Merlin is trying to create a very precise walk for Mrs. Tweedy that will reveal something about her character.

lines and Mrs. Tweedy marches into view. "It has a vast range of movements," explains Tristan Oliver. "You can program in any camera move you like and it will automatically break it down into individual frame-sized pieces so that—at the same time with absolute precision—you can animate and move the camera. When you run the finished footage it will have all the smoothness of a live-action movie and, if you need to re-shoot a scene, it is completely and accurately repeatable."

Peter and Merlin experiment with walks, up and down, back and forth. "I think it needs to be a heavy walk . . ."; "Yes, the heel should come down first, like this . . ."; "She has her hands behind her back . . ."; "She smashes her way through the gate—BAM!"; "Striding in! Boomp! Boomp! Boomp!"; "It's a dramatic entrance that is totally intimidating to the chickens!"

"It's tough getting even seemingly simple sequences right," says Merlin, as they begin a rehearsal of the animation using an enormous motion-control rig called a Milo, which is essentially "a computer-driven crane with a camera on the end." The Milo is an unwieldy monster that is nevertheless capable of infinitely subtle movements: it makes it possible to begin a shot with sunrise on the distant hills, pull back to reveal the farm, and then zoom down and into the chicken yard as the chickens get themselves into ordered

The set is raised up so that the puppets' feet can be located through holes in the "ground" of the chicken coop and secured beneath. In order to achieve animation in the crowd scenes, the animators will have to scramble about "underground" relocating a good many chicken legs. For the purposes of today's rehearsal, the animation will only be "blocked," which means that about one in every ten frames will be tried out, so as to get a rough feel of how the scene will look. Only when that blocking has been approved will the real animation begin.

Next stop is a conference with key animator Darren Robbie, who is working on the sequence in which Fowler unbends toward Rocky and hands him his much-prized R.A.F. flying badge. The discussion

Opposite: Mrs. Tweedy intimidates the ranks of nervous chickens in the scene shown in storyboards, left, drawn by Michael Salter and David Bowers. She has assembled the chickens for roll call and is about to measure Babs to see if she's fat enough to begin making pies. The puppet of Mrs. Tweedy is standing on elevated rigging so that from the movie camera's point of view, she will appear to loom over the assembled chickens.

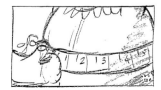

Miss Chicken Pie 1955

is being videotaped for later reference. "It's great fun," says Peter who clearly relishes the opportunity to demonstrate his undoubted talents at playacting. "More to the point, it's a really good way of explaining what you want from somebody." The scene takes place in Fowler's Hut, with Rocky entering in a defensive mood. Darren acts for Rocky, to a recording of Mel Gibson's voice: "Alright, pops. What'd I do now?" Peter as Fowler crosses the room toward the younger rooster with the elderly knock-kneed strut of a bird who is well past his prime.

A swagger stick tucked under his arm, he pulls himself up to his full height, puffs out his chest and tosses his head back: "A very brave and honorable deed, sir. In light of your actions this evening, I dutifully admit that I have misjudged your character. I present you with this medal for bravery. . . ." Peter pins an imaginary badge on Darren's chest. "And I salute you!" Taking one step backwards, Peter's right hand swings up to give a crisp salute. "In honor of the occasion, I surrender the bunk entirely. I shall sleep under the stars. . . ." Marching to the

On another set. Nick is reviewing a sequence involving several chickens and demonstrating a frantic flapping wing-or-hand movement that is a quintessentially Park gesture: the palms turned outwards, the fingers spread wide. It says anxiety and alarm, and betokens a character who is almost out of control.

178

door, he throws over his shoulder a line that will disturb Rocky deeply: "I await tomorrow's flying demonstration with great anticipation."

The soundtrack is rewound and the two men swap roles: Darren is Fowler and Peter plays the astonished Rocky.

So it goes. Peter and Nick will be on the move till the end of the day. "It's very difficult for them," says line producer Carla Shelley. "They are trapped in this strict regime and their days are, literally, micromanaged with not much free-thinking time. We tried to build 'time out' into their schedules, but all that happened was that people who knew they were free found them and pounced on them. So now we fabricate bogus meetings, put them in the schedule and then whisper quietly in their ear that they've got half an hour free—so go and disappear!"

Chicken Run has presented Peter and Nick with many challenges of which the animators are largely unaware. "The first problem," says Carla, "was the question of co-directing: neither of them had done it before. They worried about how they were going to split up the work, whether their styles were going to marry and how they were going to make a film that looked as if one person had made it."

"It's true," says Peter, "we really feared that people would 'see the join,' but you can't. Nick and I have very different sensibilities, but what we have in common is so much stronger than what makes us different." For Nick, perhaps the hardest challenge was that of giving up being a solo animator in favor of being a director. Does he miss handling the plasticine, I wondered? "Not at all," comes the emphatic reply. "I always thought I would, but I don't. I long to do it again, but not on this film." He thinks a moment and then adds candidly, "Actually, the animators have got so good, that I wouldn't *dare* do any animating on *Chicken Run*." Peter sees the funny side of the situation: "It's crazy. Neither of us have ever animated these chickens. We come up with a really difficult thing like animating chickens and we then get other people to do it for us!"

So if they're not creating the magic themselves and if the animators working for them really are better at it—although, it should be said, *they* would all deny that—then what are Peter and Nick giving to their teams? "Understanding of character, a feeling for story, a sense of pacing," says Peter. "And the big picture," adds Nick. "The big picture and the detail—and everything in between."

For Peter its like being the conductor of an orchestra. "The animators are like musicians, they are all virtuosi, they know the notes and how to play them, our job is simply to hold them all together, keep the pace in sync, give their performance the emotional beat." Nick finds another analogy. "It's like driving a team of twenty horses. They are all moving in the right direction, but everyone is pulling slightly differently, this way and that; left to themselves they might head off down any one of a number of different paths. We have to hold the reins, keep the team on course."

Whichever description you prefer, they have certainly done something along those lines, and the completion and success of *Chicken Run* will show just how well they have done it.

Doing the chicken: Loyd Price and Nick Park experiment with possible flapping gestures. By role-playing sequences with the directors in front of a video camera, the animators get the opportunity to rehearse a character's performance before animation begins.

179

Epilogue

"You know what the problem is?," Ginger asks her fellow chickens when they begin to lose interest in the idea of escaping from Tweedy's Farm, "the fences aren't just round the farm. They're up here—in your heads. Don't you realize, there's a whole world out there?"

Ginger has vision. She can see beyond the difficulties of today, to a world of hope and opportunity . . .

As in the film story, so with the filmmakers: there have been many times during the making of *Chicken Run* when the task seemed insurmountable. The idea to make an animated feature film is easily put into words, but nowhere near as easily accomplished!

As the film enters its final months of production, the number of animation units at work increases and preparations are getting underway on the creation of the soundtrack.

Sound is—and has always been—vitally important to the animated film: from the twangs, bangs, squawks, and squeaks of the early Hollywood cartoons through to the sophisticated musical scores of today's animated features.

As line producer Carla Shelley sees it, "Sound is a crucial element. You are starting with a blank canvas in animation, creating a fantasy world: and all the sounds in that world also have to be created—from scratch."

"Imagine a world before chickens—a chickenless, eggless world. . . ." NICK

"I am—and it's horrible." FETCHER

Whether it is the squish of a pair of Wellington boots crossing a muddy farmyard, the metallic rattle of a padlocked gate, the snarl of a dog, the bang of a door, or the splat of a turnip squashing against a shed wall: none of these sounds exist when the scenes are being shot.

Chicken Run has a team of sound editors each working within their own specialist area, such as dialogue or sound effects. Starting with the story reel, the editors lay down a temporary soundtrack that will give the directors a feeling for how picture and sound will work together in the completed film. Eventually, however, those sounds have to be replaced with those that will be heard in the cinema. And all of those sounds have to be created and recorded for the film.

In devising a soundscape for *Chicken Run*, Aardman are working with a local supervising sound editor, James Mather, and with De Lane Lea sound studios in London. The team includes Graham Headicar as supervising sound editor and Adrian Rhodes, who has collaborated with Aardman on many previous productions and who will ultimately mix the final soundtrack for the film.

One of their biggest challenges is going to be the pie machine. Just as much thought and planning went into designing the look of the machine, so Graham Headicar is now at work deciding how it is going to *sound*.

Graham began collating sounds for this sequence at an early stage, his aim being to create a musical, rhythmic soundtrack for the machine. One idea he is experi-

menting with is to underscore these effects with a verbal track using the words "Chicken pies! Chicken pies!" emanating as a sinister whispered mantra from the bowels of the machine.

One question, which the filmmakers wrestled with at the writing stage and which is now being grappled with anew, is the difference between the human world and the chicken world and, specifically, what happens when those worlds collide.

"Throughout the film," says Carla Shelley, "the chickens display very human behavior and speak with human voices; but how should they behave when Mr. and Mrs. Tweedy come on the scene? For example, in the learning-to-fly sequence, as soon as the Tweedys appear, the chickens start acting like *real* chickens, pecking at the ground. The question facing the sound guys is, should the chickens be *clucking*? And, if they *are* clucking, should they sound like *real chickens* clucking or like human beings *imitating* chickens?" With a few months to go, it is a question still being debated.

"The one thing we always knew," says executive producer Michael Rose, "was that the music score would be a major creative element of the film."

Throughout the production process, of course, many of the sequences on the story reel have been accompanied by a "temporary score," provided by the music editors to help establish the tone and mood for different scenes. The time has now come to commission a composer to create the score which will be heard on the finished film. Peter Lord and Nick Park choose two English composers, Harry Gregson Williams and John Powell.

Currently working in America, Harry and John collaborated with DreamWorks and PDI on their recent animated feature *Antz*. Theirs is a collaborative partnership that combines extensive feature-film experience in both animation and live action with an English sensibility that is in tune with the directors' creative vision for the film.

In January 2000, Harry and John spent two weeks at the Aztec studios with Peter and Nick and immediately got down to sketching initial themes and ideas that will become the building blocks for the eventual score.

With a great deal done, but with much still to *be* done, Peter and Nick reflect on the changes that have taken place within a company that, for many years, felt more like a family than a firm, but which is now grown to a size where it is less easy for the founders to have a personal relationship with everyone who works for them.

They know that with the success of *Chicken Run*, the future of Aardman will also change beyond anyone's expectations. Nothing will ever be quite the same again. So, how does Peter Lord view that future? "It's undoubtedly going to be marked by radical change, but the thing is, for us, radical is *normal*. Not that it isn't still shocking, but it's *normal* shocking. Everything here has been a series of challenges: the first was simply to get something—*anything*—on television; then to make a film that could tell a little story; after that we wanted to make a five-minute film; then a kids' series; a pop video, and a commercial. Next we set out to make a twenty-minute film; a *thirty*-minute film; then a *feature* film. In terms of format, there *isn't* a 'next thing'

deal" (*The Independent*)—the story is one of increased jobs and opportunities for a British company.

For the folk at Aardman it is the realization of a long-standing ambition. "For many years," says Michael Rose, "our dream was to get into long-term feature film production: to make not just *one*, but a succession of pictures."

To do anything else, as David Sproxton recalls, would have been unthinkable: "We knew perfectly well that to set up a full-blown feature studio for just one production was madness. We needed to have a rolling program of both development and production and we needed to ensure that we could do that on *our* terms."

Whilst there were plenty of potential partners in the offing, Aardman were anxious to avoid being railroaded into any long-term arrangements. David remembers: "We had been in discussions with all the major studios who wanted to lock us into a three or five picture deal from the outset. But given the length of time it takes to conceive and make a feature, this would have seemed like a life sentence with little likelihood of parole! So, our plan was to negotiate a single picture arrangement with a view to extending the deal fairly quickly, if things panned out satisfactorily."

The key then was to find the *right* long-term partner. "We needed," says Michael, "to work with a studio which would help us take Aardman's unique creativity into the features world without undermining or damaging it and

to do; so, in a way, I guess the challenge we now face is to keep it all going."

David Sproxton takes a similar view: "You can't go back. You have to go on. Everything is in a state of change all the time. What we have to address is not only what films we make next, but *how* we make them: What is the most appropriate, imaginative, creative approach to management? How can we grow and yet avoid getting massively hierarchical? How

do we address not just the expectations of the audience but also those of the staff: how do we meet their needs and wants, keep everybody motivated, and sustain everyone's morale?"

In October 1999 came the announcement that Aardman had signed a deal with DreamWorks to produce four more feature films. In Britain—where the newspapers run headlines such as "Wallace and Gromit creator in £150m Spielberg

"I guess the challenge we now face is to keep it all going," says Peter Lord

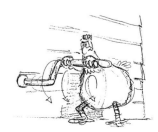

guarantee Aardman its creative and economic independence." What David was looking for was, "a unique and imaginative arrangement for a unique and imaginative studio." And Aardman were in a strong position to achieve this aim: "From a business point of view we didn't need to depend on features as our future. We are self-sufficient through the making of commercials for short-term finance, with additional benefits of long-term revenue streams through the distribution and exploitation of our character-led short films and television series, such as Wallace and Gromit and Rex the Runt. We also had a great deal to offer in the form of more than twenty years of making stop-frame films, experience which has given us an understanding of both the process and the people issues involved."

Jeffrey Katzenberg at DreamWorks responded with patience and understanding and David describes the current relationship with DreamWorks as "a good, complimentary partnership."

"DreamWorks," says Michael, "have proved on Chicken Run that they are just that partner, providing sensitive creative support and advice alongside their exceptional marketing and distribution expertise."

As far as Peter Lord and Nick Park are concerned they were reassured to discover that they had nothing to fear from being involved with a large American studio. "One of the first things we heard from Jeffrey Katzenberg," recalls Peter, "was the assurance that if we were working with him, he would be the start and the end of our chain of command. There was to be no Hollywood bureaucracy;

we wouldn't have to convince anyone else about what we were doing. If Jeffrey bought it, the studio bought it."

"Without DreamWorks' faith and trust," adds Nick, "Chicken Run would have been impossible."

And beyond Chicken Run? Aardman are already working on their second feature film—and thinking about a third (which might just possibly star Wallace and Gromit) and, beyond that, there will be another film which has yet to be thought about. . . .

"If you take a walk in the hills," says Peter Lord, "human nature is such that you climb to the top in the hope of seeing the view on the other side. But when you reach the crest of the hill, what do you find? Yet another summit beyond. For a long time we've looked at Chicken Run as the last summit, but having finally breasted it, what do we find? Another one. So the next summit is really about keeping on doing what we do. It's a more cerebral fulfillment. Supposing you have built this English studio in Bristol that, in twenty years time, is regularly producing feature films: now that would be really amazing."

As Chicken Run enters its final stages of production, a new version of Aesop's fable, "The Tortoise and the Hare," is in the early stages of development. All the old questions return to be answered, not least that of whether adapting an already known story has any appeal for a studio that has always aimed to tell its own stories. "Yes, it's a classic story," admits Peter, "but one that came to us carrying very little freight. Aesop's fable is a small, slight story so it's relatively

easy to give it our own personality, shape, and character."

"To begin with," says Nick, "we couldn't find a hook for it; we needed an original angle—then we found it." That angle was to recreate the well-known tale in an unexpected, but familiar, format: an animated documentary with vox pops, that looked back to those early Aardman series, Conversation Pieces and Lip Sync that won Aardman much praise and—with Creature Comforts—their first Academy Award.

Peter Lord is well aware of how much work will need to go into the new movie: "Feature films are such a huge achievement that I've no doubt that the next one will seem as difficult as the first one—more difficult, probably, because it will, I trust, have a very hard act to follow. I'm sure that Chicken Run will seem quite astonishing to audiences, but the fact is, you can't astonish an audience the same way twice, you have to do something different the second time around. Chicken Run is a great story, but the next one's got to be greater!"

Whether that story features chickens, tortoises, hares, all of them, or none of them, there is every reason to suppose that it will be all we have come to expect from this remarkable studio, where creativity means taking a lump of colored plasticine, shaping it and molding it into some human or animal player who can act out . . . well, anything.

GINGER: There's a whole world out there.

PATHÉ (vertical logo, left margin)

DREAMWORKS PICTURES
in association with
PATHÉ present
An AARDMAN Production

CHICKEN RUN

Cast
(in alphabetical order)

FETCHER
Phil Daniels

MAC
Lynn Ferguson

ROCKY
Mel Gibson

MR. TWEEDY
Tony Haygarth

BABS
Jane Horrocks

MRS. TWEEDY
Miranda Richardson

GINGER
Julia Sawalha

NICK
Timothy Spall

BUNTY
Imelda Staunton

FOWLER
Benjamin Whitrow

The Filmmakers

DIRECTED BY
Peter Lord and Nick Park

PRODUCED BY
Peter Lord, David Sproxton
and Nick Park

EXECUTIVE PRODUCERS
Jake Eberts, Jeffrey
Katzenberg and Michael Rose

SCREENPLAY BY
Karey Kirkpatrick

BASED ON AN ORIGINAL
STORY BY
Peter Lord and Nick Park

MUSIC BY
John Powell and Harry
Gregson-Williams

LINE PRODUCER
Carla Shelley

SUPERVISING DIRECTOR OF PHOTOGRAPHY
Dave Alex Riddett

DIRECTORS OF PHOTOGRAPHY
Tristan Oliver and Frank Passingham

SUPERVISING ANIMATOR
Loyd Price

PRODUCTION DESIGNER
Phil Lewis

MODEL PRODUCTION DESIGNER
Jan Sanger

EDITED BY
Mark Solomon

TECHNICAL DIRECTOR
Tom Barnes

PRODUCTION MANAGER
Harry Linden

ASSOCIATE PRODUCER
Lenny Young

CASTING BY
Patsy Pollock

ANIMATION

KEY ANIMATORS
Merlin Crossingham
Sergio Delfino
Suzy Fagan
Guionne Leroy
Dave Osmand
Darren Robbie
Jason Spencer-Galsworthy

ANIMATORS
Jay Grace
Will Hodge
Seamus Malone
John Pinfield
Andy Symanowski
Ian Whitlock
Douglas Calder
Stefano Cassini

ADDITIONAL KEY ANIMATORS
Teresa Drilling
Jeff Newitt
Chris Sadler
Steve Box
Tom Gasek

ADDITIONAL ANIMATORS
Terry Brain, Gary Cureton,
Mike Cottee

ASSISTANT ANIMATORS
David Bennett, Claire Billett,
Michael Cash, Martin Davis,
Curtis Fell, Jo Fenton,
Andy Fraser, Maria Hopkinson,
Kim Keukeleire, Bob Scott,
Christina Vilics

TRAINEE ASSISTANT ANIMATORS
Francesca Ferrario, Andy Spilsted,
Seth Watkins

ADDITIONAL ANIMATION
Tobias Fouracre
Mike Booth

PRODUCTION

1ST ASSISTANT DIRECTOR
Fred de Bradeny

SUPERVISING PRODUCTION
COORDINATOR
Jacky Chrisp

2ND ASSISTANT DIRECTORS
Robert Hurley
Richard Priestley

2ND UNIT 2ND ASSISTANT
DIRECTOR
Merriel Waggoner

ADDITIONAL 1ST ASSISTANT
DIRECTOR
Tony Tyrer

ASSISTANT PRODUCTION
MANAGER
Ezra J. Sumner

3RD ASSISTANT DIRECTOR
Will Norie

ASSISTANT TO PETER LORD AND
NICK PARK
Ali Cook

ASSISTANT TO DAVID SPROXTON
Ngaio Mackintosh

ASSISTANT TO MICHAEL ROSE
Julia Hardy

ASSISTANTS TO CARLA SHELLEY
Sarah Brazier, Helen Sargent

ASSISTANT TO JAKE EBERTS
Irene Lyons

ASSISTANTS TO JEFFREY
KATZENBERG
Cynthia Park, Holly Von Praagh

ASSISTANT TO MEL GIBSON
Doug Weaver

ADDITIONAL ASSISTANTS
Lisa Kelly, Julie Imboden,
Christy Yellen

RESEARCHER
Veronica Pollard

STUDIO RUNNER
Simeon Chard

PRODUCTION RUNNERS
Richard Beek, Dan Gregory,
James Heyworth, Pippa Mercer,
Liam Owen, Victoria Spurgeon,
Jennifer Thomas, Adam Loretz

ADDITIONAL 3RD ASSISTANT
DIRECTOR
Lisa Butler

STORY & SCRIPT

ADDITIONAL DIALOGUE
Mark Burton
John O'Farrell

STORYBOARD SUPERVISOR
David Bowers

STORYBOARD ARTISTS
Michael Salter
Rejean Bourdages
Dan Lane
Martin Asbury
David Soren

ADDITIONAL STORY
Kelly Asbury, Cody Cameron,
Randy Cartwright, Brenda Chapman,
Jorgen Gross, Vicki Jenson,
Robert Koo, Serguei Kouchnerov,
Damien Neary, Simon Wells,
Catherine Yuh

STORY & CONTINUITY SUPERVISOR
Bridget Mazzey

STORY & CONTINUITY
COORDINATORS
Tara Cunningham, Timothy Hogg

STORYREEL
Mark Taylor
Sylvia Bennion
David Vinicombe

SCRIPT CONSULTANT
Pete Aitkin

MODEL MAKING

Model Design

DEPUTY PUPPET PRODUCTION
DESIGNER
Anne King

DESIGN TEAM SUPERVISORS
Kate Anderson
Virginia Mason

188

DESIGN TEAM LEADERS
Claire Drewett
Harriet Thomas

Sculptors
Gavin Jones, Linda Langley,
Lisa Newport

Armatures

ARMATURE DESIGN SUPERVISOR
Simon Peeke

SENIOR ARMATURE DESIGNER
Kevin Scillitoe

ARMATURE DESIGNERS
Andrew Bloxham
Jon Frier
David Pedley

JUNIOR ARMATURE DESIGNER
Kyleigh Adrian, Phil Gray

MULTIPLE ARMATURES
John Wright, Jeff Cliff

Model Makers

MODELERS
Gill Bliss, Allan Burne,
Diane Holness, Grant Macdonald,
Lee Wilton, Kevin Wright,
John Craney, Mick Hockney

FOAM TECHNICIAN
Elinor Weston

EXTRA LARGE SCALE PUPPET WORK
Mackinnon & Saunders

MOUTH & BEAK REPLACEMENT
COORDINATOR
James Moore

Model Production Team

MODEL DEPARTMENT PRODUCTION
MANAGER
Lizzie Spivey

PUPPET COORDINATOR
Sheila Clarkson

PUPPET MAINTENANCE COORDINATOR
Rebecca Levine

PUPPET WRANGLER
Kate Wadsworth

PRODUCTION ASSISTANTS
Louise Atkinson, Nada Backo

MODEL RESOURCES MANAGER
Kerry Evans

WORKSHOP MANAGERS
John Adams, Johnny Parsons

Costumes & Textiles

SENIOR COSTUME DESIGNER
Sally Taylor

TEXTILES DESIGNERS
Shane Dalmedo, Nicola O'Toole,
Jane Whittaker

TEXTILES JUNIOR
Janine Chisholm

TEXTILES DEVELOPMENT
Jo Conrad

Painting

PAINT DESIGN SUPERVISOR
Polly Holland

SENIOR PAINTER
Michelle Freeborn

PAINTERS
Arlene Arrell, Peter Atkinson,
Lorraine Mason, Ruth Mitchell,
Cat Russ

ASSISTANT PAINTER
Nikki Armstrong

Mould Making

MOULD MAKING SUPERVISOR
Rob Horvath

MOULD MAKERS
Jim Connolly, Matt Pilston

Press Moulds

PRESS MOULD COORDINATOR
Helen Schell

PRESS MOULDS
Alison Evans
Marguerite Fry
Tina Klemmensen
James Parkin

ASSISTANT
Will Becher

Multiples

MULTIPLES SUPERVISOR
Graham G. Maiden

MULTIPLES MODEL MAKERS
Gideon Bohannon, Michael Hares,
Claudia Hecht, Nigel Leach,
Jemma Proctor, Mark Waters,
Liz Watt

MULTIPLES ASSISTANTS
Sarah Owen, Colin Ventura

ART DEPARTMENT

ART DIRECTOR
Tim Farrington

ADD'L PRODUCTION DESIGNER
Roger Hall

ASSISTANT PRODUCTION DESIGNER
Matt Perry

ASSISTANT ART DIRECTOR
Trisha Budd

ADD'L ART DIRECTOR
Rosalind Shingleton

ADD'L ASSISTANT ART DIRECTOR
Julie Philpot

PROPS SUPERVISOR
Jane Kite

LAYOUT GRAPHIC ARTIST
Darren Dubicki

GRAPHIC ARTIST
John Davey

SET DESIGNER
Alastair Green

DRAUGHTSPERSON
Jo Smith

CG ARTIST
Steve Blake

COORDINATOR
Bee Arnoux

DESIGN RESEARCH
Paul Gough

**Sets and Props by
Farrington Lewis**

SET PRODUCTION SUPERVISOR
Jon Minchin

SET CONSTRUCTION
SUPERVISOR/LEAD ENGINEER
Jak Goodyear

SET PRODUCTION COORDINATOR
Libby Watson

ACCOUNTS ADMINISTRATOR
Tanya Booth

Team Leaders

SETS AND PIE MACHINE
Mike Applebee

SETS, FLYING MACHINE & CAD
John Pealing

PIE MACHINE
Roddy MacDonald

LEAD ENGINEER, PIE MACHINE
Mark Plenderleith

Fabricators

FABRICATORS
Mike Bass, Andy Brown,
Anthony Gould, Mike Gould,
Mark Gunning, Mathew Healey,
Patrick McGrath, Martin Norie,
Jes Par, Steve Priddle,
Martin Rolfe, John Smith

SPRAY SHOP
Terry Hathway

RUNNERS
Cliff Lewis, Cecily Pearce

Set Dressing

SENIOR SET DRESSERS
Maria Hopkinson
Lizzy New Bones
Manon Roberts

SET DRESSERS
Justine Bailey
Rachel Bowen
Kitty Clay
Anita Clipston
Melanie Ford

Models and Props

TEAM LEADERS
Cathy Price
Jo Weeks

MODEL MAKERS
Craig Atkinson, Claire Baker,
Georgie Everard, Nancy Jones,
Duncan Miller, Damian Neary,
Lesley Osbourne, Bridget Phelan,
Gavin Richards, John Smith,
Ed Sams, Clay Saunders,
Lisa Scantlebury, Richard Webber,
Kathy Williams, Ruth Wynne

Scenic Artists

HEAD OF PAINTING
Sue Black

SENIOR PAINTER
Francesca Maxwell

SCENIC PAINTER
John Fattorini

PIE MACHINE PAINTER
Mahali O'Hare

**Pie Machine and Flying Machine
by Farrington Lewis**

189

Additional Specialist Props & Vehicles by Jeff Cliff Model Making
Lincoln Grove
Robert Jose
Emma Jay
Nick Hudson
Nikki Armstrong

John Wright Modelmaking
Adrian Sims, Dave Weaver,
Richard Andrew, Kenny Monger,
Roger Whiter, Steven Elford,
Ann Wright, Georgie Everard

Toblerone imagery used with kind
permission of the rights owner

EDITING
ASSOCIATE EDITOR
Angharad Owen

FILM EDITORS
Robert Francis
Tamsin Parry

ASSISTANT EDITOR
Andrew Ward, Jo Bale

ADDITIONAL EDITING
Vicki Hiatt, Yoke Van Wijk,
John Carnochan,
David McCormick

TRAINEE
Yvonne Davies

PRODUCTION ASSISTANT
Adrian Shipp

TRACK BREAKDOWN
Jane Hicks, Hilary Wyatt

PROJECTIONIST & ENGINEER
Roger Sharland

PROJECTIONIST
Zbigniew Trzaska

CAMERA
LIGHTING CAMERAMEN
Simon Jacobs
Andy Mack
Paul Smith

1ST ASSISTANT CAMERA
Robert Dibble

SUPERVISING CAMERA ASSISTANT
Toby Howell

CAMERA ASSISTANTS
Jon Gregory
Janet Legg
Beth MacDonald

Jeremy Hogg
Charles Copping
Richard Whiteford

JUNIOR CAMERA ASSISTANTS
Andy Mitchell
Churton Season

MOTION CONTROL OPERATORS
Linda Hamblyn
Willy Jason Marshall

MOTION CONTROL TRAINEE
George Milburn

LIGHTING
SUPERVISING GAFFER
John Bradley

GAFFER
Ian Jewels

BEST BOYS
Richard Hosken
Adam Vernon

LIGHTING DEPT COORDINATOR
Carl Hulme

SENIOR ELECTRICIAN
Andy Loran

ELECTRICIAN
Paul O'Bryan

ADDITIONAL ELECTRICIANS
Tim Fletcher
Jon Graves

WIREMAN
Peter Sim

RIGGING
SUPERVISING RIGGER
Del Lawson

SENIOR RIGGERS
Alan Scrase
Nick Upton

RIGGERS
Craig Atkinson
Andy Brown

ASSISTANT RIGGER
Alan Barrett

TECHNICAL
ELECTRONICS DEVELOPMENT
ENGINEER
John Morrissey

MECHANICAL DEVELOPMENT
ENGINEER
Alan Gregory

ELECTRICAL ENGINEER
Bob Gregory

COMPUTER ENGINEER
Neil Baker

TECHNICAL RESOURCES
COORDINATORS
Katherine Mann
Chiara Minchin

VIDEO & MECHANICAL ENGINEER
John Oaten

ENGINEER & WIREMAN
Kevin Yates

AVID SUPPORT
Malcolm Smale, Adam White

CAMERA CONVERSIONS
Doug Fries, John Buckley

CAMERA SUPPORT
David Cox, Alex Porter

FINANCE
PRODUCTION ACCOUNTANTS
Karen Walter
Alex Matcham

FINANCE DIRECTOR
Lisa Bilbe

FINANCE CONTROLLER
Kerry Lock

PRODUCTION ACCOUNTS ASSISTANT
Derek Connop

ACCOUNTS ASSISTANT
James Flintoff, Sara Edwards

PAYROLL ADMINISTRATOR
Josie Marshall

ADDITIONAL ACCOUNTS ASSISTANTS
Tom Bannister, Simon Hill

SOUND
SOUND RE-RECORDING
Adrian Rhodes

SOUND EDITORS
Graham Headicar
James Mather

DIALOGUE EDITOR
Tim Hands

SOUND FX EDITOR
Danny Hambrook

ASSISTANT SOUND FX EDITOR
Lee Maturine

ASSISTANT DIALOGUE EDITORS
Dan Laurie
Simon Price

ASSISTANT RE-RECORDING MIXERS
Howard Bargroff
Stuart Hilliker

FOLEY RECORDING ASSISTANT
Terry Isted

FOLEY ARTISTS
Jack Stew
Diane Greaves
Ben Jones

FOLEY RECORDING MIXER
Ted Swanscott

TRAINEE ASSISTANT FOLEY EDITOR
Alistair Chant

SOUND RECORDING
De Lane Lea Studios

ADR CONTRACTOR
Brendon Donnison, Lyps Inc

MUSIC
MUSIC SUPERVISOR
Marylata E. Jacob

SCORE RECORDED AND MIXED BY
Nick Wollage

SCORE RECORDED AND MIXED AT
Abbey Road Studios, London

MUSIC EDITORS
Richard Whitfield
Dina Eaton

ADDITIONAL MUSIC
Steve Jablonsky
James McKee Smith
Geoff Zanelli

ORCHESTRATIONS
Bruce L. Fowler

MUSIC PREPARATION
Tony Stanton

ORCHESTRA AND VOCAL
CONTRACTOR
Isobel Griffiths

MUSIC PRODUCTION SERVICES
Thomas Broderick
Gretchen O'Neal

POST PRODUCTION
POST PRODUCTION SUPERVISOR
Mike Solinger

POST PRODUCTION EXECUTIVE
James Beshears

NEGATIVE CUTTER
Jason Wheeler

COLOUR TIMER
Peter Hunt

SENIOR LABORATORY LIAISON
Paul Swann

**VISUAL EFFECTS BY
COMPUTER FILM COMPANY**

DIGITAL VISUAL EFFECTS SUPERVISOR
Paddy Eason

VISUAL EFFECTS PRODUCERS
Rachael Penfold
Drew Jones

SUPERVISING CG ANIMATOR
Dominic Parker

VISUAL EFFECTS LINE PRODUCER
Fiona Chilton

COMPOSITING ARTISTS
Mark Nelmes, Alex Payman,
Gavin Toomey, Adrian de Wet,
Matt Kasmir

CG ANIMATORS
Richard Clarke
Justin Martin

DIGITAL PAINT ARTISTS
Ian Fellows
Robert Hall
Sule Bryan-Hurst

VISUAL EFFECTS EDITORIAL
Tabitha Dean
Natasha Wilkinson
Roz Lowrie

**DIGITAL CONFORM AND GRADING
BY CFC DIGITAL LAB**

PRODUCER
Jan Hogevold

DIGITAL GRADING
Tom Debenham

DATA SUPPORT
Darrel Griffin

SCANNING AND RECORDING
Merrin Jensen, Adam Glasman,
Steve Tizzard, Scott Marriot,
Julia Egerton

DANCE SEQUENCE

DANCE CONSULTANTS
Ann Peskett, Graham Puckett,
Jesse Newton, Norman Newton,
Katherine Wyatt

PUBLICITY & PHOTOGRAPHY

PUBLICIST/MARKETING
Arthur Sherriff

PUBLICITY UNIT MANAGER
Clare Thalmann

ASSISTANTS
Adam Barriball, Lottie Storey

PHOTOGRAPHERS
Tom Barnes, Mark Chamberlain,
Simon Jacobs, Richard Laing,
Paul Norris

SONGS

"Flip Flop and Fly"
Written by Charles Calhoun and
Lou Willie Turner

"The Wanderer"
Written by Ernest Maresca
Performed by Dion
Under license from EMI-Capitol
Music Special Markets

WITH SPECIAL THANKS TO

Penney Finkelman Cox
Cecil Kramer

The Staff of Aardman
All at Pathé

Andy Birch
Marty Cohen
Bruce Daitch
Ann Daly
Leslee Feldman
Nick Fletcher
Art Frazier
Michael Kahn
Simon J. Smith

Note: The final credits for Chicken
Run were not available when this
book went to press.

**SPECIAL THANKS TO THE
FOLLOWING PEOPLE FOR THEIR
INVALUABLE CONTRIBUTION TO
THIS BOOK:**

Corinne Antoniades, Adam Barriball,
Tom Barnes, Grace Chen,
Alison Cook, Kristy Cox,
Bernard Furnival, Frances Harkness,
Vicki Hart, Eric Himmel,
Liz Keynes, Lisa Murphy,
Loyd Price, Michael Rose,
Carla Shelley, Tracey Small,
David Sproxton, Lottie Storey,
Sharron Traer, Clare Thalmann,
Walter de la Vega, and Libby Watson.

PHOTOGRAPH CREDITS:

Tom Barnes: 9, 10, 11 (both), 12, 13,
20-21, 29 (top right), 29 (bottom
left), 34-35, 36, 37 (bottom), 39
(both), 40 (top), 41, 43, 44-45, 46, 47
(left), 48, 51, 59, 60, 61, 65, 82-83, 86,
87, 88, 89, 101, 115, 116, 117, 123, 127,
132, 138, 143, 144-45, 147, 151, 153
(top), 158, 159 (bottom), 160 (top
right), 160 (bottom left and center),
161, 165, 170, 175, 176-77, 180-81, 182,
185, 187.

Stuart Freedman: 16 (top left and
right), 84, 108 (bottom), 110
(bottom right), 114 (all), 119 (center
right), 164.

Simon Jacobs: 25, 37 (top), 79, 81, 119
(center right), 126 (bottom), 129, 133
(both), 136-37, 142, 153 (bottom), 162
(both), 163, 166, 172, 178, 179.

Richard Laing: 2, 17, 105, 106-107, 108
(top three photographs), 109 (all),
110 (center right), 112 (bottom), 113
(bottom), 122, 126 (top), 167 (top),
173.

Andy Maccormack: 160 (bottom
right).

Rob McEwan: 7, 94 (right), 95 (left).

The puppets illustrated on the
following pages are seen as posed
for Chicken Run's marketing
program: 24, 31, 38, 50, 63, 78, 92,
103, 104, 110, 119, 124, 156, and 183.

Drawing by W. Heath Robinson,
page 32 (left), © The Estate of Mrs.
J. C. Heath Robinson. Drawing by
Rube Goldberg, page 32 (right),
Rube Goldberg is a registered
trademark and copyright of Rube
Goldberg Inc.